Eel

Animal
Series editor: Jonathan Burt

Already published

Crow
Boria Sax

Ant
Charlotte Sleigh

Tortoise
Peter Young

Cockroach
Marion Copeland

Dog
Susan McHugh

Oyster
Rebecca Stott

Bear
Robert E. Bieder

Bee
Claire Preston

Rat
Jonathan Burt

Snake
Drake Stutesman

Falcon
Helen Macdonald

Whale
Joe Roman

Parrot
Paul Carter

Tiger
Susie Green

Salmon
Peter Coates

Fox
Martin Wallen

Fly
Steven Connor

Cat
Katharine M. Rogers

Peacock
Christine E. Jackson

Cow
Hannah Velten

Duck
Victoria de Rijke

Shark
Dean Crawford

Swan
Peter Young

Rhinoceros
Kelly Enright

Horse
Elaine Walker

Elephant
Daniel Wylie

Moose
Kevin Jackson

Forthcoming

Hare
Simon Carnell

Spider
Katja and Sergiusz Michalski

Pig
Brett Mizelle

Pigeon
Barbara Allen

Camel
Robert Irwin

Chicken
Annie Potts

Wolf
Garry Marvin

Penguin
Stephen Martin

Ape
John Sorenson

Butterfly
Matthew Brower

Sheep
Philip Armstrong

Eel

Richard Schweid

REAKTION BOOKS

Published by
REAKTION BOOKS LTD
33 Great Sutton Street
London EC1V ODX, UK
www.reaktionbooks.co.uk

First published 2009
Copyright © Richard Schweid 2009

Printed and bound in China

British Library Cataloguing in Publication Data
Schweid, Richard
    Eel. – (Animal)
    1. Eels
    I. Title
    597.4'3

    ISBN: 978 1 86189 423 6

Contents

Introduction

Here's to the eel.

This book is a portrait of that amazing and slippery freshwater fish found in the rivers of North America and Europe. It
is an animal with a fascinating natural history, and humans
have eaten it for thousands of years. It is not the infamous electric eel, which lives in the headwaters of the Orinoco and
Amazon rivers, nor the moray eel, that vicious marine predator,
nor one of the other more than 400 other species of eel that are
known around the world. The freshwater eel is a snake-like fish,
covered in slime and without sharp teeth, hunkered down at
home in the muddy bottom of some slow-moving body of fresh
water – a river, lake, pond or creek. Surprisingly, the life cycle of
this torpid, freshwater fish is one of the most astonishing on the
planet, and remains one of the animal world's great unsolved
mysteries. It has challenged naturalists and biologists since
Aristotle first conjectured about eel reproduction more than
two thousand years ago.[1] Chapter One examines what we *do*
know about the eel's natural history and how we know it.

All the eels in all the rivers of both North America and
Europe are believed to be born in the same area of the Sargasso
Sea, which is a million square miles of water within the Atlantic
Ocean, between Bermuda and the Azores, bounded by strong
currents. It is believed to be the only place where American and

European eels are born. The eels hatch in the southern part of the Sargasso as larvae and are carried by the currents to either Europe or North America, a journey that can cover thousands of miles and take over two years. They enter a river as glass eels and develop into fully formed baby eels called elvers, then into adults. The continent they end up on will determine which of two closely related species they will belong to. The larvae entering European rivers are *Anguilla anguilla* and those that enter North American rivers are *Anguilla rostrata*. Although the two are genetically different, they are nearly identical, with the only observable difference being the number of vertebrae (114 in the case of the European eel, 107 in the American).[2] The eel's average lifespan is thought to be 10–15 years, but eels in captivity have lived 55 years. Freshwater eels are called yellow eels until they mature sexually and change into silver eels, in which form they return down river to the ocean, then on to the Sargasso Sea where they will spawn and die.

The survival of both species appears to be threatened. As chapter Two explains, wild stocks are in precipitous decline.[3] The hypothetical culprits are over-fishing, reduced habitat,

An adult eel.

fresh-water pollution and changing climatic conditions. Viable American or European eels have never been bred in captivity and the population comes exclusively from larvae born in the Sargasso. It has become clear over the past decade that the number of baby eels (glass eels) entering the world's rivers is decreasing dramatically, and there is widespread agreement among scientists that European and American eels face a serious threat to their continued existence.[4] The problem is not one that is immediately evident, because the grown eels that people are most likely to cross paths with are still plentiful. These are eels that entered fresh water as glass eels up to fifteen years ago. It is only in recent years that the numbers of larvae entering rivers appears to have fallen so drastically. Although no one knows why larvae choose to enter any given river, what is clear, around the world, is that many fewer are doing so. Scientists generally believe that this means that fewer larvae are hatching in the Sargasso. From the St Lawrence river in Canada to the Chesapeake Bay in Maryland and from the River Bann in Northern Ireland to the River Po and the wetlands of Comacchio on the coast of northern Italy, glass eel recruitment is decreasing year by year. Explanations for what is causing this decline are varied. Should stocks continue to fall, and aquaculture efforts continue to fail, eels could rapidly disappear.

Eels and people have interacted for millennia, and have a rich mutual history. Ancient Egyptians are said to have worshipped them,[5] and the Greeks revered them on their tables. They have long been held in high esteem as food around the world. A favourite on English tables ever since people began keeping records of what they ate, eels were one of the founding foods of the United States, the first food that the Native Americans showed the Mayflower pilgrims how to find, thus saving them from starvation.[6] The Japanese currently constitute the largest market for them, consuming huge quantities annually, and they are considered a delicacy in many European countries, while jellied eels are still available on the streets of London at a price even the poor can afford, and stewed eel with mashed potatoes remains a popular choice for lunch in one of London's many surviving pie and mash shops.[7] Total eel consumption in Northern Europe alone, in 1998, was around 10 million kilograms (22 million lb) a year, according to *Aquaculture Magazine*,[8] and annual eel sales around the world are estimated at about $2 billion, the great bulk of which is destined for Japan.

The beginnings of the relationship between humans and eels are explored in chapter Three, from classical Greece up through the Middle Ages. The eastern Mediterranean is a long way for a larva to come from the Sargasso Sea, given the number of fish and birds that would be glad to eat it before it arrived. Still, the rivers of Egypt, Greece, and Rome all held eels and each of these civilizations accorded a different treatment to the fish.

In Western Europe people first began recording what was served and eaten, along with recipes for preparing those dishes, in the thirteenth century. The earliest cookbooks included ways to prepare eel, and it was clearly a common and much-appreciated food. The arrival of the Industrial Age did nothing to diminish people's appetites for it. What's more, the English colonists who arrived in the New World depended in great part on the eel to feed them. That it is an ancient food in the Americas was evident from reports of the earliest missionaries. Native Americans fished for and ate eel in a variety of ways. Chapter Four examines the history of its nutritive interaction with humans in the United Kingdom and the United States up to the twentieth century.

Chapter Five examines the way in which people have fished for eels since time immemorial. While many anglers today would rather catch pneumonia than an eel, others still find them good sport and good eating, and actively seek them out. In addition, the global market for eels sends many people out to fish for them commercially, and they constitute Europe's largest inland fishery.[9]

Chapter Six examines the uses to which eels have been put down through the centuries (culinary ones apart), including literature, art and apparel. While eel consumption has virtually disappeared in the United States, the fish is still widely relished in Europe and the Asian market is immense. However, the natural resource is diminishing rapidly. High demand and low supply are conditions that would seem to provide a context for the development of a lucrative aquaculture. And that would be the case, if only the eel was not so finicky about where it is born, so difficult to make comfortable in artificial conditions. Despite vast expenditures of time and money, eels steadfastly refuse to reproduce viably in captivity. The only way to farm eels is to buy glass eels captured in the wild and raise them to table size.

Finless eels at a restaurant in Guangzhou, China.

Moray eel.

In 2000 over 90 million kilograms (200 million lb) of eel were eaten in Japan, worth about $1.8 billion at that year's exchange rate.[10] The Japanese eel mimics the American and European eels in its life cycle, with its own equivalent of the Sargasso Sea: the Asian larvae drift on what the Japanese call the Kuroshio current, entering the rivers of China, Korea and Japan. They are thought to hatch out about 1,200 miles south of Japan, in an area called the Ryukyu Trench.[11] A substantial number of eels (*Anguilla japonica*) have always entered Japan's rivers, but they are not nearly enough to feed the Japanese appetite. Plenty of incentive exists for substantial research investment. The Japanese, with their limited territorial waters and their tremendous appetite for fish, have a highly advanced and sophisticated aquaculture industry. A lot of time and money has gone into attempts to reproduce eels that will thrive and grow to table size. Researchers have succeeded in harvesting eggs from female eels and fertilizing them artificially. Larvae have hatched, and turned into glass eels, but no one has successfully raised numbers of them to a harvestable size.[12] The person who is eventually successful at reproducing eels that will eat and thrive in captivity stands to make a lot of money. As it is, large facilities where baby eels are fattened to market size exist in a number of countries, including China, Japan, Denmark, Holland, Italy and Spain, but all the eels they raise were born in the wild and captured after they turned from larvae into young eels. Well over 11 million kilograms (25 million lb) of eel were caught around the world in 2000, for instance, all of which came from wild stock.[13] Chapter Six takes a look at the current market for eels, the development of eel aquaculture and what its prospects might be for the future.

The eel and its life cycle have intrigued observers of our natural world since people started looking around them. Just to watch an eel is a pleasure. They may be slimy, and live in the mud, but they have a wonderfully sinuous grace, and the same capacity to fascinate us as the snakes they resemble. Hopefully this book will provide a glimpse into the remarkable world of an eel.

Anguilla L'Anguille.

Cum priuil. Regie. 8

1 The Eel Question

What creatures swim in secret depths below?
Unnumbered shoals glide thro' the cold abyss
Unseen, and wanton in unenvyed bliss.
For who with all his skill can certain teach,
How deep the sea, how far the waters reach?
Oppianus, second century CE[1]

The mysterious and remarkable life cycle of eels has fascinated and baffled observers ever since people began recording natural histories of the animals and plants around them, and over two thousand years of study has produced remarkably little data with which to answer the most basic unknowns about an eel's existence. The situation is still much as a German marine biologist named Leopold Jacoby described it, writing from Berlin in an article reprinted in a report from the US Commission of Fish and Fisheries in 1879:

> To a person not acquainted with the circumstances of the case, it must seem astonishing, and it is certainly somewhat humiliating to men of science, that a fish which is commoner in many parts of the world than any other fish ... which is daily seen at the market and on the table, has been able in spite of the powerful aid of modern science, to shroud the manner of its propagation, its birth, and its death in darkness, which even to the present day has not been dispelled. There has been an eel question ever since the existence of natural science.[2]

That existence is generally agreed to have begun with Aristotle, the first natural historian, who addressed the eel question around

Eels in an etching by Albert Flamen (c. 1620–after 1693), a Flemish artist based in France who specialized in natural history subjects.

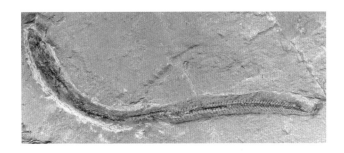

An eel fossil from Lebanon, near the town of Byblos. The red in the fossil is fossilized blood.

350 BC in his *Historia Animalium*. That's a long time to study an animal and still know next to nothing about it. Never has an animal been investigated for so long, bought, sold and eaten in such quantities, and remained so little known. Most fish with a high market value have had their lives and their genomes carefully picked apart and reproduced in artificial environments, their life cycles as familiar and easy to manipulate as a potato's. Although salmon is one of the few other fish in the world that lives in both fresh and salt water, eels are in many ways their opposite. Eels are catadromous, meaning they are born in salt water, live in fresh water and return to the ocean to spawn and die. Salmon, on the other hand, are anadromous: they are born and die in fresh water, living their lives at sea. They are majestic. The sight of a large airborne salmon, its body arched in a leap as it makes its way upriver against rapids bears little resemblance to the lazy, slime-covered eel buried in the mud of that river. For all their wild, energetic beauty, salmon are currently bred like cows or pigs, condemned to lives as monotonous and hemmed in as that of calves in a feed lot, or chickens living their entire lives in the shadowy, anxious interiors of factory farms. A huge global demand for eels has also created an important market, but the key to reproducing eels in captivity has yet to be found. Eels live their lives on their terms, or not at all.

Many people in Europe or the USA never see a live eel during their lifetimes. Those who *do* come in contact with one will usually find it in the middle of adulthood, in its yellow-eel phase, a snake-like fish living in the mud of fresh-water rivers, ponds, lakes and creeks. In that context it seems the most ordinary of creatures with an unremarkable life. However, the known facts, as they are pretty much universally accepted today among marine biologists and naturalists, prove that all eels in all the rivers of eastern North America, and all the eels in European rivers, are born in the Sargasso, in the area popularly known as the Bermuda Triangle, located roughly between the Azores and Bermuda. They have made what seems an impossibly long journey to arrive at that small bit of mud at the bottom of some slow-moving body of fresh water.[3]

At least, this is what today's marine biologists and naturalists tell us, although adult eels have never been seen swimming, reproducing or dying in the Sargasso. In fact, live adult eels have never been seen there at all. The only two adult eels ever located in the Atlantic Ocean were dead, found in the stomachs of other fish. The eel's migration back to its birthplace, and what it actually does when it gets there, is believed to take place far below the surface, and as of the year 2009 was still completely unobserved. However, the eel larvae, the leptocephalae found in the Sargasso, are so small that it is certain they are born nearby. Larvae measuring as little as 5 centimetres (2 inches) could not have been drifting for long, and such small larvae have never been found anywhere else.

An eel's life consists of distinct phases, radically different from each other. The first is as a larva that will eventually leave the ocean for fresh water, at which point it is called a glass eel because it is has no pigmentation and is a virtually transparent, tiny wriggling ribbon. As it begins swimming upriver it becomes an elver, with pigmentation, although it may still not be longer than 6.5 centimetres (2.5 inches). The elvers swim up the river on the flood tides, and hunker down near the bottom when the tide is going out. Eventually the elvers transform into young adult eels, known as yellow eels. They have a greenish-yellow-brown hue and golden eyes. In the final, sexually mature and reproductive phase of its life, an eel turns gun-metal blue, with enlarged, bright blue eyes and a thicker skin. These are referred to as silver eels.

The larvae of the American and the European eels are virtually identical, shaped like small oval leaves, and called leptocephali. They are believed to hatch from fertilized eggs at substantial depths in the Sargasso – possibly as far down as 300 metres (1,000 feet) or more below the surface. That strange surface, where sargassum seaweed floats in giant clumps, and marine life is relatively scarce and simple. The same stretch of water in which Christopher Columbus's ships were marooned, and where his crews went nearly crazy with the stillness and boredom, the dreaded horse latitudes where so little breeze blew that Joshua Slocum wrote in 1900 about being becalmed there and being able to read on deck at night by the light of a candle, with not even a breath of wind to flicker the flame.[4]

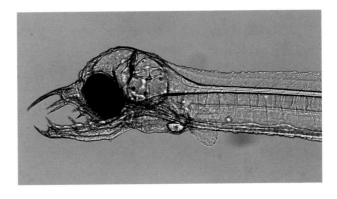

A 12-day-old larva eel. The eyes and mouth are fully developed, and it is ready to start feeding on its own.

The leptocephali rise from the depths where they hatch out, attracted by the light at the surface. Once there they drift with the Sargasso's strong currents. At the beginning of their journeys, they measure only a few centimetres and are leaf-thin, and if they wind up going to a European river they have an unimaginably difficult journey of years ahead of them. Numerous fish and birds will try to eat them if they get a chance, and no one knows exactly how the larvae nourish themselves as the current carries them along. Some hold that their primitive digestive system allows them to ingest and expel tiny organisms on the surface, while others posit that they are nourished through their skins in some manner. What is certain is that they are feeding, because during the long drift they continue to grow. By the time they reach the northernmost point on the Sargasso's currents they are as long as 8 centimetres (3 inches).

Eventually, they feel the pull of one or another river as they drift close to the coasts of either Europe or North America, and they head for fresh water. By the time they reach brackish water, where fresh and salt water mix, the leptocephali have narrowed and lengthened into thin, transparent noodles, hardly wider than a hair, with a pair of eyes like black dots at one end – glass eels. Research indicates that when it comes to choosing a river to enter from the sea, glass eels are not drawn to the river where their parents spent their lives. What it is that *does* draw a glass eel to a given river remains a mystery. European eels enter rivers ranging from the Atlantic coasts of Britain and Ireland to rivers emptying into the Mediterranean, just as their North American cousins may opt for entering fresh water anywhere from Georgia to Nova Scotia.

No one knows what signals the eel larvae to transform their bodies into these hair-like ribbons and begin the process of physical changes necessary to go from salt water to fresh. As if it

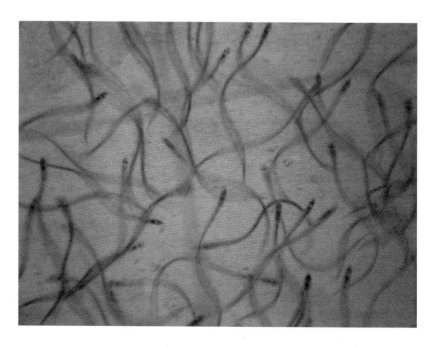

Glass eels in a holding tank.

is not enough that this tiny creature has spent months adrift at sea, it must now transform itself, and adapt to a drastic change on a cellular level. It is at this moment when the eel's natural history takes on its rare and shining beauty. Metamorphosis is a sensation not included in the repertoire of things humans can possibly experience during their lifetimes. Eels enjoy a variety of physical experiences for which our lives provide no analogies.

From the estuaries and mouths of the rivers, the tiny eels frequently continue upstream, particularly the females who sometimes go great distances inland. Reports are not uncommon of eels hundreds of miles from a coast.[5] Having come thousands of miles, across an ocean and up a river, what tells an eel that one particular bit of muddy bottom will do quite nicely for home? No one knows. Whatever it is, it's clear to an eel. Once established in its territory, the fish is not likely to stray more than 90 metres (100 yards) away for the next ten or twenty years. It will hunt things like insects, snails, crayfish and rotting flesh by night, take it easy in the mud during the day, and will grow up to 1 metre (3 feet) long.

Finally, its brain registers another signal, one that sends the eel back to the Sargasso to mate, a last long journey, the third and final huge transformation in the life of an eel. They will leave their freshwater homes and head back downstream. The sexually mature eels feed voraciously, and change colour from the muddy yellow/green of adult eels to a darker green on top and snow-white on their bellies. Now they are silver eels. They will swim downriver in the autumn, and when they reach brackish water they will pause, completing the physical transformation to prepare them for their months-long journey, as once again they change form, habit, cells and skin.

By the time eels have swum downriver and arrived in estuarine waters, they will have eaten heavily and will be about 28 per cent body fat. This is the stored energy that will power their trip back to the Sargasso. Now their digestive systems will atrophy. The eels will never eat again. Once they mate, with what remains of their energy after the long voyage back, they will die. In preparation for re-entering the ocean, their bodies go through profound changes. The pupils of their eyes expand and turn blue. They will need a new sight in the depths of the sea, where there is little light. They will also go through osmosis, a change in blood chemistry that allows them to go from bearing some 14 lb of fresh-water pressure per inch on their bodies, to supporting over a ton of ocean pressure per inch 6.4 kg/over 1,000 kg. Once these changes are accomplished, their time of hanging around brackish water is over. It is time to start out on the long swim back to the Sargasso, propelled by a single-minded pull, unimaginable to us in its fixity. The Sargasso's force draws eels back to it as surely as iron to a magnet. Once they reach the Sargasso the females will produce eggs for the males to fertilize, and then the exhausted adults die.

While eels have never been observed reproducing in the Sargasso, they have never been seen doing so at any other place in the wild either. The watershed moment for acquiring what little knowledge we have, or think we have, about the eel's life cycle was when the Danish marine biologist Johannes Schmidt pulled the first larvae from the Atlantic Ocean in 1904. Schmidt spent the rest of his life considering the eel question. Many others had done so before him. Some of history's most illustrious observers, ranging from Aristotle to Sigmund Freud, speculated in print about the mechanics of eel reproduction.

Aristotle's first systematic look at the natural world, in which it was valued for itself, categorized and treated as an entity apart from the human, had lots to say about the eel, a favourite food of the ancient Greeks. He correctly observed that, unlike most fish that live in both fresh and salt water, eels are cata-dromous, and he determined that spontaneous generation from the earth was the most likely explanation for how eels reproduced:

> Eels are not produced from sexual intercourse, nor are they oviparous, nor have they ever been detected with semen or ova, nor when dissected do they appear to possess either seminal or uterine viscera; and this is the only kind of san-guineous animal which does not originate either in sexual intercourse or in ova . . . Some persons have thought that they were productive, because some eels have parasitical worms, and they thought that these became eels.

This, however, is not the case, but they originate in what are called the entrails of the earth, which are found spontaneously in mud or moist earth.[6]

It is not difficult to discern Aristotle's frustration at the lack of observable facts, his sense that he is missing something and that his conjectures, which would set the eel apart from all other animals, are erroneous. The fact is, as he noted, even on close inspection an eel does not appear to have any reproductive organs and it was this more than anything else that led to millennia of mistaken ideas about eel reproduction.

In addition to the difficulty of locating the eel's genitalia, confusion grew out of other mistakes made over the centuries by some of the most important minds of their times. In the thirteenth century the Dominican monk and scholar Albertus Magnus insisted in his *On Animals* that the eel gave birth to live young. This notion of the eel as viviparous was given added currency when dissected eels were revealed to have intestinal parasites, which observers often mistook for foetal

A heron devouring an eel, as depicted in a medieval manuscript.

Whoever takes an eel by its tail or a woman at her word can be said to have nothing; etching by the Bolognese artist Giuseppe Maria Mitelli (c. 1634–1718).

CHI PIGLIA L' ANGVILLA PER LA CODA, E LA DONNA PER LA PAROLA PVO DIR CHE NON TIEN NIENTE.24

Chi le speranze sue fabrica, e fonda
Di fede feminil soura la base,
Getta i suoi fondamenti à l'Aura, à l'Onda.

Reynard the Fox stealing an eel from a fish-wagon, illustrated in a medieval manuscript.

Eel and frog in a stream with bulrushes; a German woodcut book illustration, 1490.

eels, exactly as Aristotle had warned. Others who published confidently that the eel was viviparous included the great Dutch naturalist Antonie van Leeuwenhoek in 1692 and Linnaeus, the Swedish botanist and taxonomist, who insisted in the mid-eighteenth century that eels were born alive from the mother's womb, even though reliable observations to the contrary had already been published. The Italian scientist and man of letters Francesco Redi was one of the first people to study parasitology. In his studies of parasites in fish, he saw that what some held to be foetal fish were only parasites living inside the eel. He began to get interested in the whole eel question, and set to work on it. In 1684 he published his conclusions that the female eel returns downriver to the sea, and once there lays her eggs.

These hatch in the spring and the elvers head upriver. He spoke to fishermen in Pisa who caught them from the city's bridges using giant sieves, and who reported catches in the spring of 1662 of over a tonne (2,200 lb) of glass eels in five hours. Redi got it right.[7]

However, he was long in the grave by 1777, when the ovaries of a female eel were finally located. Credit for this discovery went to Carlo Mondini, an Italian biologist and professor at the University of Bologna, some 20 miles from one of the greatest eel grounds in Europe, the Po River delta around the town of Comacchio on Italy's north-eastern coast. Mondini is most famous for having anatomically described a malformation in the inner ear that causes a relatively common form of deafness. His report of 1791, 'The Anatomic Section of a Boy Born Deaf', was widely read, and the inner-ear condition is now called Mondini's deformity. His name was also given to the female eel's ovaries, often referred to as the organ of Mondini. His

Eel on cement floor.

discovery that the frilled ribbons inside a female eel's abdominal cavity were ovaries, not fringes of adipose tissue, as had been previously believed, was monumental for our understanding of eels.[8] If there was a female sexual organ, the analogous male equipment would also eventually be found. What was clear, finally, with this discovery, was that the eel was a fish and reproduced just like every other fish in the world, despite Aristotle's assertion to the contrary.

Through the centuries, both before and after Mondini's description of the female's ovaries was published in the late eighteenth century, observers often seemed to be competing with each other to elaborate the most outlandish explanations of how eels reproduce. The first best-selling writer about fishing, Izaak Walton, whose book *The Compleat Angler* was published in 1653 and is still in print today, held fast to the theory that eels were viviparous. 'The eel is bred by generation . . . her brood come from within her . . . I have had too many testimonies of this to doubt the truth of it myself . . . If I thought it needful I might prove it, but I think it is needless.'[9]

Testimonies regarding eel reproduction were plentiful, and not to be trusted. It was commonly believed among English country folk that eels grew from the hairs of horses' tails falling into the water. As late as 1862 David Cairncross, a chief engineer and factory manager in Dundee, published a slim volume in London that was the distillation of a lifetime of eel observation, called *The Origin of the Silver Eel*. He claimed to have discovered an 'eel beetle' and to have proven that these insects spend the first part of their lives in the form of a beetle, and the latter part as eels.

When it begins life, the land animal's nature prevails,
and when it ceases to breed it alters its form to the fish

Eel (*Anguilla rondeletius*), from Johann Kaup's *Catalogue of Apodal Fish in the Collection of the British Museum* (1856).

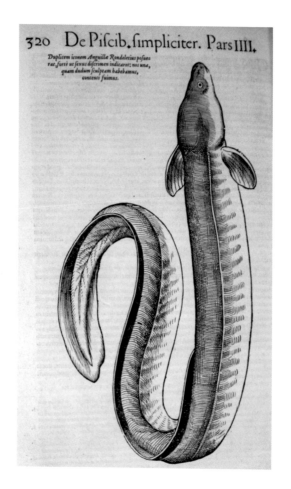

320 De Piſcib.ſimpliciter. Pars IIII.

Duplicem iconem Anguillæ Rondeletius poſue rat, forté ut ſexus diſcrimen indicaret: nos una, quam dudum ſculptam habebamus, contenti fuimus.

nature. It is evident, however, that the eel in the early stages of its career, even in the water, is to some degree tinged with the beetle nature, for I have seen them out on the edge of the loch in search of food, but after they are older they never leave the water . . .[10]

The idea that a beetle is the progenitor of eels was not confined to Cairncross's curious mind. In 1879 Leopold Jacoby wrote: 'it seems incredible, and is nevertheless a positive fact, that the Sardinian fishermen consider a beetle, the *Dytiscus Roeslii*, as the procreator of the eel. They very generally call this beetle "Eel-mother".'[11]

It was not until almost a century after Mondini's discovery that such speculations were finally put to rest. In 1874 a Polish naturalist named Szimon Syrski, who was the director of the museum at the University of Trieste, announced that he and his team had finally found the male reproductive organs, although even then the exact location of the testes continued to be a mystery.[12]

A number of eminent scientists worked on pinpointing the site, and one of them was Carl Claus, Sigmund Freud's advisor and head of the Institute of Comparative Anatomy at the University of Vienna, where Freud was a medical student. He sent Freud to Trieste in 1876 to review Syrski's work and see if he could find eel testicles. Freud failed to do so. After dissecting some 400 eels, the man who was later able to uncover something as hidden as our own subconscious had to admit defeat. 'I have been tormenting myself and the eels', Freud wrote, 'in a vain effort to rediscover [Syrski's] male eels, but all the eel I cut open are of the gentler sex.'[13]

In 1897 an Italian biologist from the University of Messina in Sicily, Giovanni Battista Grassi, and his assistant Salvatore Calandruccio, captured a sexually mature male eel in the Straits of Messina and were able to finally identify its gonads. The looped, frilled ribbon had been seen before, but not identified as the testes. In this eel it was full of milt. Now the fish-ness of the eel was proven beyond a doubt, the reproductive organs located, but a lot remained unknown.

Leptocephali had been described as early as 1856, when the German naturalist Johann Kaup wrote about a larva from the Straits of Messina, but he considered it a new species, and baptized it *Leptocephalus brevirostris*.[14] Forty years later, and a year before they would locate the male eel's gonads, Grassi and Calandruccio made their other great discovery. The straits of Messina are particularly turbulent waters and at certain times of the year powerful currents meeting from the north and south churn up the sea and deposit the bodies of a variety of fish species, which normally live at great depths, on the beaches. It was here that Grassi and Calandruccio observed numerous specimens of Kaup's *Leptocephalus brevirostris*, the thin, flat creature with a tiny head and two black dots for eyes. They wondered if this could not be the larval form of some other animal rather than a fully grown animalcule, as Kaup had believed. It was known that the number of muscle segments in a larva was the same as the number of vertebrae in the resulting fish into which the larva transformed. They counted the number of myomeres (skeletal muscle tissue segments) in the larvae and found 115, then began looking for a match among fishes. They found it in *Anguilla anguilla*'s 115 vertebrae and nowhere else. To prove their hypothesis they raised a larva in an aquarium and documented its transformation to glass eel, and then to eel. Finally someone had put an end to tales of beetles and horsehairs. 'The abysses of the sea are the spawning places of the Common Eel', wrote Grassi in his 1896 report to the Royal Academy of Rome. 'Its eggs float in the sea water . . . I am inclined to believe that the elvers ascending our rivers are already one year old.'[15]

News of the results of this marvellous bit of human deduction had circumnavigated the eel world by the end of 1896. However, the pair of Italian scientists went too far in their desire to see the eel question fully resolved. They also concluded that the Straits of Messina were the birthplace of all European eels, ignoring the fact that all the larvae they had found appeared to be fully grown, with none smaller than 60 millimetres (2.4 inches), and most already beginning the process of changing into glass eels.

That was where scientific understanding of the eel question stood at the end of the nineteenth century. Still unanswered was the puzzling question of where the eel was coming from.

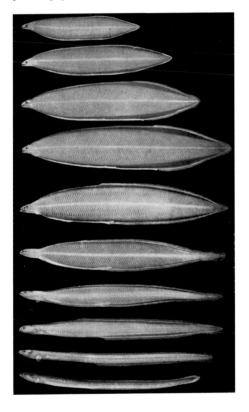

Development of the eel from larva to the glass eel, shown by Johannes Schmidt in 1924

Where did the leptocephali hatch out? Here is where the eel world's most dedicated investigator, Johannes Schmidt, took centre stage. A young Danish marine biologist, he was hired on to a Danish team in 1902 to work on a programme called International Investigations of the Sea. One of the programme's goals was to examine the larval stages of food fish. For that purpose a steamer named *Thor* was equipped with trawling equipment and collection facilities and when it sailed in 1903 Schmidt was aboard. In the second year of its investigations, 1904, a 7.5 centimetre (3 inch) eel larva was captured in a trawl that took place in the north Atlantic, between the Faroe Islands and Iceland. This was the first recorded instance of a leptocephalus found in the Atlantic, and it confirmed Schmidt's doubts about Grassi's conclusion that eels were born in the Mediterranean. In subsequent trawls between Iceland and the Breton coast of France hundreds of larvae of this size were netted. Schmidt published his first findings in 1906 in a report to the International Investigations of the Sea Commission.

By then he was wholly committed to solving the eel question, certain that he was on the verge of discovering the birthplace of both European and American eels. He severely underestimated what lay ahead, he wrote, looking back some twenty years later:

I had little idea at the time of the extraordinary difficulties which the task was to present, both in regard to procuring the most necessary observations and in respect of their interpretation . . . The task was found to grow in extent year by year, to a degree we never dreamed of; in fact, we have been obliged, in order to procure the necessary survey material, to make cruises of investigation ranging from America to Egypt, from Iceland to the Cape Verde Islands. And this work has been handicapped throughout by lack of suitable vessels and equipment and by shortage of funds . . . [16]

In those twenty years Schmidt went through four large ships in his collecting efforts and relied on numerous other Danish ships to provide him with samples. As early as 1911 he was recruiting commercial transatlantic Danish vessels to help him, providing them with the necessary equipment to make short trawls during the course of their voyages and preserve any leptocephali yielded by the nets. Between 1911 and 1915 over 500 hauls had been made by 23 vessels, and some 120 larvae were collected. As Schmidt charted these hauls it became evident that the farther south they occurred, the smaller the larvae captured. He reasoned that the smaller the larvae, the closer their birthplace.

Schmidt's fortunes, however, ran hot and cold. In 1913 things had been looking up and he felt confident that he was closing in on the elusive eel birthplace. A Danish transport company provided him with a two-masted schooner, the *Margrethe*, to equip as a research vessel. In the fall of 1913 he directed the schooner toward the West Indies, trawling as he went. The results were exciting. The larvae grew more numerous as he moved from east to west and north to south, conforming to his hypothesis. And they were progressively smaller, many of them only 3.5 centimetres (1.5 inches) long. 'This placed it beyond doubt that the stock of eels in Europe must have its origin in an area situated far to the west in the Atlantic Ocean,' he recounted.

The plan was to spend the winter at St Thomas, and then to fill the return voyage to Denmark with more trawls. Unfortunately the *Margrethe* ran aground on an unnamed West

Indian island and sank. Fortunately the onboard collection of specimens was saved. Schmidt described what happened next: 'On returning from the West Indies we set about endeavouring to get another schooner to work in place of the *Margrethe*, but then came the great war and all plans for further researches at sea had to be laid aside . . . several of the vessels which had been assisting us were sunk by submarines.'

As soon as the war was over Schmidt began trying to raise funds for another trawling expedition. The Danish traders of the East Asiatic Company provided him with a four-masted, 500-ton motor schooner, *Dana*, and by 1920 Schmidt was once again trawling nets through the western Atlantic. Eventually, in the Sargasso, he was hauling out leptocephali that were less than 1 centimetre (0.5 inch) long. 'These are so tiny that there can be no question of their having moved any considerable distance from the spot where the eggs were spawned,' he wrote.

At the same time that Schmidt was moving to resolve one mystery, another was unexpectedly arising. As early as 1913, on board the ill-fated *Margrethe*, he had noticed that both American and European eels appeared in his catches.

> It was with mingled feelings that we noted this fact, since it involved a further complication of the eel question, which at this point seemed more intricate than ever. Technically, also, it increased the difficulty of our investigations, since the only means whereby the larvae of the two species can be distinguished one from the other is by counting, under the microscope, the 104–120 myomeres in each individual specimen – a very lengthy and laborious business, especially on a small vessel at sea.
>
> After the cruise of the Dana, in 1920, I looked upon the matter in quite a different way. True the technical difficul-

ties have not diminished – I have in mind the counting of myomeres in the thousands of specimens obtained on the cruise – but the comparison of the life history of the two species which our investigations have allowed us to make, is to my thinking one of the most interesting chapters in the history of the European eel . . .[17]

Some marine scientists speculate that in prehistory the American and European continental shelves were joined in the middle of the Atlantic. The eels may have all belonged to a single species. When the shelf went through a tectonic shift and widened into a huge divide, the eels evolved into two species. This theory is bolstered by the fact that hybrid American-European eels have been discovered in the rivers of Iceland.[18]

The larvae of the American eels that Schmidt caught were generally larger than the European eels from the same area. He concluded that they were hatched in the same places, but because they needed to spend less time in the ocean to mature and move into fresh water, they grew faster than the European eels. The American eel larvae would go through their transformations into glass eels and enter fresh water while their European cousins might not even be halfway through their marine drift. The last piece of the leptocephali puzzle fitted into place in Schmidt's mind, and he could confidently draw maps and write descriptions of the general migration of the larvae to both continents.

By 1924 he had narrowed his search for the birthplace down to a small area of the Sargasso. After twenty years of trawling the Atlantic looking for leptocephali, he was ready to publish and prove his conclusions. Schmidt's tireless research did much to answer the mysteries of the eel question, but he was the first to acknowledge that many gaps were left in our knowledge. He wrote of the journey undertaken by European eels as they

Ribbon eel in Fiji.

returned down river and out to sea, beyond the reach of eel traps or fishing fleets.

Fresh conger eel on a British market stall.

No longer subject to pursuit by man, hosts of eels from the most distant corners of our continent can now shape their course southwest across the ocean, as their ancestors for unnumbered generations before them. How long the journey lasts we cannot say, but we know now the destination sought: A certain area situate in the Western Atlantic, northeast and north of the West Indies. Here lie the breeding grounds of the eel.[19]

We know far less about most of the other 600 or so species of the world's eels belonging to the order of Anguilliformes.

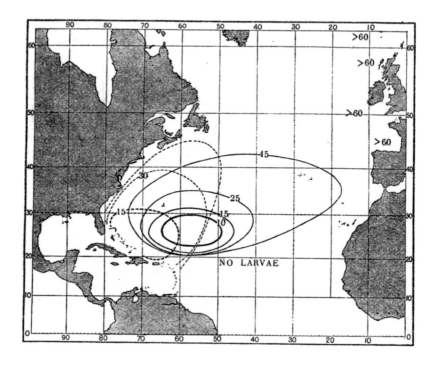

European and
American eel
breeding areas
and larvae
distribution
(dotted line
represents the
American eel,
continuous line
the European),
diagrammed by
Johannes Schmidt.

Virtually the only other eels with which Europeans have had frequent contact have been the conger, *Conger conger*, and the moray, *Muraena helena*. The former is still highly regarded in Europe as food, although its flesh has a considerably different texture and taste from that of the freshwater eel. The moray was highly regarded by the Romans, who were recorded as keeping them in pools until they brought them to the table, and were said to have occasionally fed disgruntled or troublesome slaves to these fish. Another fish of which people think when they hear the word eel is the so-called electric eel, which is not an eel at all, but is more closely related to a carp. Around the globe, eels are sighted, eaten, but rarely understood.

Johannes Schmidt mapped the leptocephali's migration, and other scientists have filled in the adult's freshwater life, but so far the critical stage in the eel's reproductive cycle, the return journey back to the Sargasso, is still wholly unobserved in the ocean. Schmidt made huge advances in our understanding of the eel's life cycle and it was reasonable to expect that the few missing pieces of the puzzle would be filled in rapidly. It has not turned out that way, partly because Schmidt's dedication to his subject has not been duplicated. No one else has come along with the ability and desire to pass their careers steaming around the Atlantic Ocean looking for eels. While a certain small number of marine biologists around the world specialize in eel, no one to date has marshalled the resources and dedicated the time to the question that Schmidt did.

Expeditions have been but rarely mounted, and those have not been particularly fruitful. In 1979 the German eel expert Friedrich-Wilhelm Tesch, whose 400-page book *The Eel* is considered the definitive work on the animal's biology, attempted to track sexually ripe silver eels released into the North Sea. They

Dana 1, one of the four research ships for Johannes Schmidt's eel investigations, 1903–22.

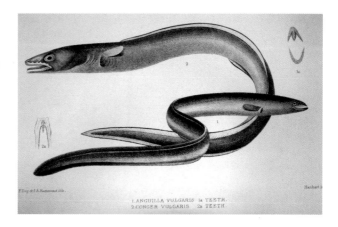

Anguilla Vulgaris, Conger Vulgaris, from Francisci Willughbeii Armig's *De Historia Piscium Libri Quator* (1686).

headed south toward the Sargasso at a depth of about 700 metres (2,300 feet), and were soon lost.[20] A decade later, in 1989, one of the United States' leading eel scientists, James McCleave from the University of Maine, directed an expedition to the Sargasso on a boat carrying sophisticated sonar equipment. The idea was to find and track adult eels, but none were found.[21]

'I think trying to catch them at sea is a bit problematic', McCleave reflected more than a decade later. 'Maybe we were being a bit naive. Perhaps the best thing to do, if you had an unlimited amount of money, would be to develop transmitters that were small enough so you could put them on fish and they'd communicate to your ship or satellite, so you could track them and find out how deep they swim, what routes they use, and how long it takes to reach their spawning grounds.'[22]

In the spring of 2007 Martin Castonguay, who did his PhD work under McCleave, and now works for the Canadian Department of Fisheries and Oceans, directed a trawling expedition with the same goal and using much more sophisticated sonar equipment. The equipment had improved but the results

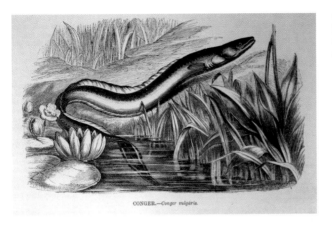

were the same: nothing. It is not surprising. It's a big ocean and the eels are, theoretically, swimming deep. As part of a simultaneous investigative expedition led by Danish researchers, eels were implanted with just the sort of device McCleave had imagined, a transmitter that would signal a satellite, which in turn would signal another ship, directed by the Danish marine biologist Henrick Sparholt. They released nineteen migrating, sexually mature eels into the sea off Northern Ireland late in the winter of 2007, implanted with lightweight electronic tags to transmit signals. Seven of the group were never heard from but signals from the other twelve were picked up. Six months later, as they headed to the Sargasso to trawl for adult eels, the ship's signals from the implanted eels indicated that they were still far north of the Sargasso. 'They only made it about a third of the way,' Sparholt told *Insight* magazine. 'So either they use a year and a half instead of half a year to reach the Sargasso Sea from Europe or the tags' extra water resistance was too much for the eel and they have been lagging behind the eel with no tags. We don't know – yet.'[23]

It has been over eighty years since Schmidt published his watershed report and answers to the eel question remain elusive, with some of the most important phases of its life still poorly understood, or not understood at all. Now some experts are warning that the species is in danger of disappearing before we even have all the answers to the eel question.

2 Endangered Eel

How mobile, fleet, and uncontroll'd,
Glides life's uncertain day!
Who clings to it, but grasps an eel,
That quicker slips away.
Konrad Gesner (1516–1565)[1]

Johannes Schmidt's description of the eel's life cycle in the ocean is still accepted today and, in fact, precious little has been added. What scientists have learned a lot more about, since Schmidt's day, is the behaviour of the eel once it transforms into a glass eel and makes that sharp left or right turn to ascend a river in the US or Europe. This has a lot to do with the relative ease of studying a creature in a river or a pond, rather than a vast ocean. Most favourable of all is the incredible fact that having travelled so far to reach its freshwater home, once an eel settles into a specific bit of mud at the bottom of a pond or creek or river, it will spend anywhere from two to twenty years there without straying further than a couple of miles from home. Finally, sexual maturity will impel the eel to swim back to the ocean, but before that it will spend a long time in one place and be relatively easy to study.[2]

Eels are hermaphroditic when they turn inland, capable of developing into either gender.[3] Those that stay in the brackish water develop male sexual organs and grow to only about half the size of those that ascend the rivers and become females. Some of those that do head upstream cover remarkable distances, while others seem more inclined to travel at an amble. In general Friedrich-Wilhelm Tesch believed the eel to show less single-mindedness and focused drive in its migration than a

Yellow eel.

salmon or other anadromous species.[4] Nevertheless, it is capable of travelling great distances for a year or two before finally settling in somewhere. An eel's sense of direction is a remarkably refined one. Studies show that not only will an eel pass its adult freshwater life in the same place, if she is captured and carried many miles away before being released she is likely to find her way home. In 1995 scientists captured sixteen eels in a river in Maine and moved them 10–17 kilometres (6–10.5 miles) away, some above where they were captured, some below. Within a few days nine of the sixteen had returned to the capture site, three more were well along the way to it and four had disappeared.[5] In other experiments Tesch noted that eels have returned to capture sites from as far away as 100 kilometres (62 miles). Their homing ability is one more confirmation of the remarkable directional system an eel has, which some of Tesch's research suggested might be based on magnetic fields. 'Laboratory experiments have shown that both silver eels *and* yellow eels are capable of following a fixed compass direction despite the removal of all hydrographical direction stimuli. This choice of direction can be influenced by altering the earth's magnetic field', wrote Tesch in 1977.[6]

Eels are nocturnally active, going out to hunt at night, willing to eat any kind of flesh that crosses their path. Once the evening's hunting is done, what they want is a safe place to pass the day, secluded and resting in as deep shade as possible, in the mud or under some sunken bit of debris.[7] When water temperature falls below 14°C (57°F) eels become dormant. Their appetites disappear and they enter a kind of semi-hibernation. They are not generally believed to dig burrows, but they do like to be inside something and seek out shelter when they can, curling up inside anywhere they can fit. They also like to have contact with one another, frequently sharing an improvised shelter or tunnelling down in the mud together. Tesch reported instances of groups of eels clustered together in huge balls 2 metres (6.5 feet) across,[8] and glass eels in the laboratory will gather in this way.

As soon as the water warms eels spend their waking hours looking for food or eating it. Since Schmidt's time, marine biologists and their students have opened up the stomachs of thousands of eels and have a good idea of what constitutes a meal for them: crayfish, snails, minnows and mussels, water striders and mayfly nymphs, caddis fly eggs and midges.[9] One thing that limits what an eel can eat is the shape of its head and mouth. Brian Crawford, an eel fisherman who wrote a book called *Catch More Eels* in 1975, reported finding 'frogs, mice, and even birds' in the stomachs of eels he'd caught over a lifetime of fishing for them.[10] Eels have blunt, reptile-shaped heads with a small mouth and an underslung jaw, the sort of skull that would look more at home on a turtle or a snake than a fish. The jaws are powerful, and lined with small, raspy teeth that can scrape but are not able to cut well. Sometimes, when an eel has caught something too large to swallow whole, it will grasp the prey in its mouth and begin to spin around the axis of its own body, tearing away flesh as it does so. An article in *Natural History* reported captive eels spinning their supremely supple bodies at 14 rotations per second.[11]

Eels prefer their food alive but if it is recently dead they will accept it. They have a reputation as devourers of carrion, but the fact is that they refuse to eat anything rotten. They will, however, eat each other, at least in the laboratory,[12] and a lot of eels have been brought into a lot of laboratories. In fact, as it is easier to study eels in fresh water than in the ocean, so they are easier still to study in a laboratory, rather than in the wild where an eel is just about the most unconfined creature imaginable. To grasp an eel is as hard as holding a handful of water. They move with a sinuous agility and are incredibly slippery. All that is left in your hand is a slime that clings to skin or clothing and is hard to wash off. The slime is thought to protect the eel against bacteria, as well as conserving moisture in its body and prolonging the length of time it can live out of water. A great deal is known about those facets of an eel's life such as diet, body structure

A fully-developed eel and the beetle that gave birth to it, depicted in *The Origin of the Silver Eel* by David Cairncross (1892).

and organs, things that can be revealed by its behaviour in a laboratory setting or by observing it under a microscope.

What scientists now know is that the eel is a highly tuned being, with one of the most acute senses of smell on the planet,[13] and a sensitivity to environmental conditions that is surprising in an animal that lives in the mud and is covered with slime. They have also concluded, recently, that the common eel may be in real and imminent danger of extinction. It is unanimously agreed among people who study such things that the eel population is shrinking drastically in many places. Fewer glass eels are arriving at and entering the rivers, and fewer eels are leaving to migrate to the Sargasso and reproduce. Most of those people who have studied eels over the past decades are issuing urgent warnings.[14]

Among the first studies to sound the alarm regarding the American eel was one by Martin Castonguay and others in 1994, which reported that between 1985 and 1992 there was an 81 per cent decline in the number of yellow eels reaching Lake Ontario.[15] Castonguay was James McCleave's student at the University of Maine, and went on to work with the Canadian government's environmental ministry. In 1985 935,000 juvenile eels were counted migrating to the lake; in 1994 that number was down to 8,000. Follow-up studies have confirmed Castonguay's initial findings and shown that between 1994 and 2004 things continued to grow worse. In 1982 a daily mean of more than 25,000 eels were using the eel ladder at a dam on the upper St Lawrence river, in Cornwall, Ontario. By 2005 that number was down to around 200. Virtually no migration was taking place and in 2006 the eel was proposed for addition to the official list of Canada's endangered species.[16] While the decline elsewhere was not as precipitous, it was steep, with a 50 per cent decline for the same time period in the Chesapeake Bay.[17]

MURÆNA.—*Murœna Helena.*

Muraena Helena. For anyone who cares about the survival of the American eel these numbers are cause for deep concern. In 2004 the Atlantic States Marine Fisheries Commission (ASMFC), representing fifteen Atlantic coast states from Maine to Florida, asked the United States Fish and Wildlife Service (USFWS) to undertake a study and make a determination as to whether *Anguilla rostrata* deserved a place on the USFWS's list of endangered species, and protection as such under the law. In 2005 the USFWS ruled that enough biological evidence existed to warrant a full-scale review of the situation. In March 2007 the Service completed its status review with the conclusion that the American eel is not an endangered or threatened species. While acknowledging that numbers are declining for reasons that are not entirely known, a USFWS spokeswoman commented, 'The eel population as a

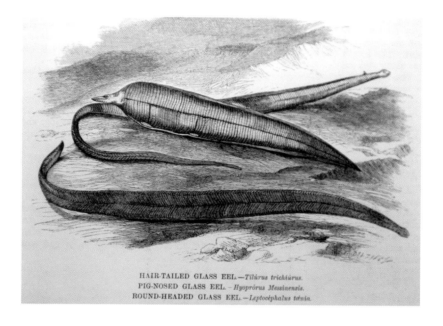

HAIR-TAILED GLASS EEL.—*Tilúrus trichiúrus.*
PIG-NOSED GLASS EEL. – *Hyoprórus Messinensis.*
ROUND-HEADED GLASS EEL.—*Leptocéphalus tænia.*

whole shows significant resiliency. If we look at eels over time, we see fluctuations in the population numbers, so a decreasing number of eels right now does not necessarily forecast an irreversible trend.'[18]

Hair-tailed glass eel, pig-nosed glass eel, round-headed glass eel.

Explanations for the precipitous eel population reduction run the whole gamut from those who echo the idea that it is part of a cyclical fluctuation to those who believe European and American eels are under assault from various combinations of factors, including pollution and habitat reduction in their freshwater phase, and climate change effects in their marine stages. Is the population decline caused by pollution in the rivers, streams, lakes, creeks and ponds where eels are found? Living in a muddy bottom in areas where agricultural runoff is heavy may affect them biologically. Or is it one more small side-effect of climate change, something altered somewhere along the great migratory route that threatens their continued existence? And it is always possible that a disease is decimating their numbers – eels are particularly vulnerable to the nematode *Anguillicola crassus*, which affects the eel's swim bladder and eventually kills it.[19] Or is the reduced number of eel larvae across the world nothing more than a routine cyclical downturn?

Eel is one of the fattiest fish, what scientists call 'lipid rich'. It spends its adult years building up a fat reserve in anticipation of an eventual return to the Sargasso, during which it will not eat, only swim. The eel's high fat content is responsible also for a great deal of its highly prized flavour. True eel aficionados hold that the best ones are those with so much body fat that their meat need only be rubbed on the bottom of a skillet to provide enough grease in which to cook them.[20] Unfortunately, this same fat accumulates heavy metals and organic chlorides. In addition, eels spend a lot of time in the mud, which is where toxins and contaminants are particularly likely to concentrate.

In 1997 Castonguay and his team published the results of their studies into the effects of contaminants like polychlorinated biphenyls (PCB) and other organochlorine pesticides.[21] Their paper reviewed the history of experiments looking for correlations between high levels of these contaminants in eel tissue and deformities or pathological lesions in those same animals, and detailed their own experiments with St Lawrence eels. The article concluded that significant contamination existed: 'American eel (Anguilla rostrata) from the St Lawrence River are heavily contaminated with chemicals that may be associated with increased incidence of disease and reproductive impairment.'

Tissue concentrations of PCBS and chlorinated pesticides were ten to a hundred times higher in silver eels captured at

Kamouraska, in the St Lawrence estuary, than in eels from a control tributary that was free of pesticides. Contamination by these pollutants could have a number of negative results, including vertebral malformations, lesions, carcinomas and undeveloped gonads. Chronic exposure to these industrial and agricultural contaminants could affect mortality, growth rates, fecundity, offspring survival and vulnerability to disease and parasites. Any of these could seriously reduce the numbers of eels making a successful journey to the Sargasso mating grounds. The same has also proven true for European eels, which have also been found to contain high levels of PCBS and organochlorine compounds.[22]

Another remarkably sensitive part of an eel, which might be affected by pollution, is its nose. Or noses. They have two, four nostrils in all, a pair at the front of their head and another pair just beneath the eyes. They constantly suck water through these nostrils, and the information they extract from it is highly sophisticated. Tesch found that an eel could still smell five bloodworms – one of its favourite foods – after they had been ground into a fine powder and diluted in 667 million litres (176 million gallons) of water. Their olfactory sensibility is ahead of almost every other animal in the world, except dogs, and per-haps living in a highly polluted body of water affects them in such a way as to interfere with their reproductive cycles. Tesch wrote: 'The eel's extremely refined sense of smell . . . has led to the assumption that the eel uses its olfactory organs not only to locate food but also to locate different places . . . Indeed, the ori-entation of glass eels toward fresh water is thought to be a form of orientation by smell.'[23]

When a larva decides to leave the ocean, the choice of a river may not always be optimal, but there will be no turning back. Human intervention has made a lot of formerly hospitable eel

Eel on a river bed,
from Wood's
*Illustrated Natural
History.*

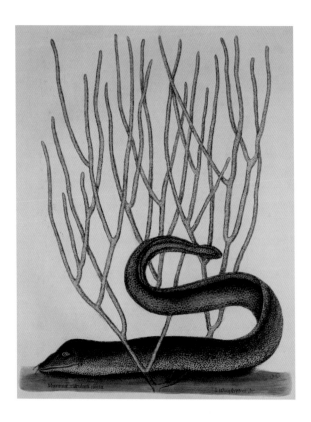

waters into places an eel cannot pass through, but it will die trying. The reduction of wetlands in general, and the construction
of dams in particular, has done for a lot of eels. While some
dams make provisions for some kinds of fish, salmon ladders
do not help eels climb, and many other dams are entirely
without provisions for any migrating fish. Many eels perish at
the dams. In its 1999 report on the status of American eels, the
ASMFC estimated that in the North Atlantic states, Maine to
Connecticut, the eel had lost access to 91 per cent of its habitat

over the course of the twentieth century, with an 88 per cent loss in those rivers from New York to Virginia.[24]

In addition to the dangers of going upstream, the dams also present a serious threat to a sexually mature female when she decides to begin her long downstream journey to reach the Atlantic. Mortality in the turbines of hydroelectric dams is high, as the silver eels try to pass through, and a 2003 study in Massachusetts showed that as many as 50 per cent of migrating eels might die in turbines, with many more being injured and in all likelihood unable to reach the Sargasso and reproduce.[25] In Maine, for instance, some rivers have at least eight hydroelectric dams with turbines that eels must swim through before reaching salt water.[26] However, it is also true that all American eels come from a single breeding population, and as long as they have some rivers that they can safely enter and leave, their overall numbers should stay healthy – they may fluctuate, but they will maintain the population in the long run. A trend currently exists towards un-damming rivers and while habitat reduction remains a threat, it is not particularly threatening to the continuation of the species.

The outlook may be less sanguine, though, if the crash in the eel population is due to something happening to affect the down-river part of the migration cycle. Perhaps fewer numbers are reaching sexual maturity, or perhaps fewer are arriving at the Sargasso Sea. And once they arrive perhaps something has gone wrong in the reproductive process. It is also possible that changed oceanic conditions have affected the percentage of larvae able to survive the trip to fresh water. Climate change is expected to alter things like sea-surface temperatures, the strength of currents and the vertical mixing of the water. All of these are things that have a bearing on the lives of leptocephali (as they do on the lives of human beings). Not only do currents and water temperature affect the larvae themselves, but they also alter the makeup of the fauna with which the larvae may have to interact, both those things the leptocephali digest and those that digest leptocephali.

A study in 2003 showed a correlation between oceanic conditions in the North Atlantic and glass eel recruitment.[27] Since no one knows the limits of what a larvae can survive on its drift north, and how precise that drift must be in order for it to arrive at a river, it is difficult to quantify the impact a changing ocean will have on the eel population. That there will be an impact, however, stands to reason. 'Glass eel recruitment depends on favourable speed and direction of currents (for transport) and suitable conditions for egg hatching and larval survival (temperature, food abundance)', reported the Gulf of Maine Council on the Marine Environment. 'Variation in oceanic conditions may help explain variation in recruitment to coastal rivers. Long-term trends in oceanic conditions, either natural or human-influenced (i.e., climate change), could profoundly affect American eels.'[28]

The ASMFC issued an official stock assessment in 2006 stating that *Anguilla rostrata*'s numbers were at or near record low levels. From 1994 to 2004 the yellow eel population in Chesapeake Bay declined by 50 per cent and in Canada's Lake Ontario by 99 per cent. The ASMFC report warned: 'Should the decline in the yellow eel indices represent a coast- or species-wide phenomenon, then there is a real risk that spawning stock biomass has also declined. If these declines are due to an unsustainable rate of total mortality (combined effects of fishing, habitat loss and degradation, dams, climate, and disease) recruitment failure is a possible consequence.'[29]

The same warning was issued in Europe, where the Joint European Inland Fisheries Advisory Commission reported their conclusions, including indications that glass eel recruitment was down by as much as 99 per cent, to 1 per cent of what it had been twenty years before:

> The Working Group, after reviewing the available information on the status of the stock and fisheries of the European eel, supported the view that the population as a whole has declined in most of the distribution area, that the stock is outside its safe biological limits and that current fisheries are not sustainable. Recruitment is at a historical low and most recent observations do not indicate recovery. Opportunities for protection and restoration of spawner escapement are fading.
>
> Earlier reports indicate that anthropogenic factors (e.g., exploitation, habitat loss, contamination, and transfer of parasites and diseases) as well as natural processes (e.g., climate change, predation) may have contributed to the decline. Measures aimed at recovery of the stock are well known and may include control of exploitation, restocking of recruits and restoration of habitat (including access to and from).[30]

By 2007 William Dekker of the Netherlands Institute for Fisheries Research was writing in one journal, 'the European eel stock is dangerously close to collapse. Without better, coordinated assessments and an international management plan, the future looks bleak for these ocean travellers.'[31]

All the possible culprits involved in the disappearance of the American eel are also cited as potential explanations for its disappearing European cousin. Again, no one can definitively say where the problem originates. What is certain is that a problem exists. At about the same time as the USFWS was deciding whether or not to put the American eel on the endangered species list, the European Union was studying what it should do about the rapidly diminishing number of *Anguilla anguilla*, both adults and glass eels.

Loss of habitat is frequently cited as a prime cause of population reduction, in Europe as in North America, but even in places where that is clearly not the case the prospects are discouraging. Take Northern Ireland's Lough Neagh, one of Europe's largest freshwater lakes, and its most important adult eel fishing grounds. The Lough's eels enter the River Bann as glass eels from the North Sea and make their way 26 miles upriver to the lake. People have caught them there for millennia. Today it is the largest wild eel fishery in Europe. About 350 families make up the Lough Neagh Fishermen's Cooperative, which controls all the Lough's eel fishing and produces about 700 tons (636 tonnes) a year. The stock of eels is carefully monitored by the Cooperative. They work actively to assure that the numbers of eels they take out of the Lough on their long lines of 1,200 hooks baited with earthworms is balanced by the number of glass eels arriving.

A congeries of eels illustrated in Alfred Brehm's *Tierleben*, a mid-19th-century encyclopaedia frequently revised and reprinted.

Two men in Comaccio, Italy, with a catch of eels.

Left on their own, elvers would need at least a year and a lot of luck to make their way 26 miles up the river to the Lough. The fishermen try to make the journey as easy as possible for them, trapping them at the river's mouth and trucking them to the lakes. Many of the baby eels get by the traps and head up-river, and for these the cooperative's members make eel ladders where a low falls interrupts the river, in just the same manner as people have made them in that spot for many centuries. A huge rope of braided straw, laid down along the water's edge, quickly becomes damp, and provides the glass eels with a means to ascend and continue forging toward the Lough. For all the assistance rendered by the fishermen, the numbers of elvers entering the Bann has fallen steadily since 1983. By 2007 Cooperative

Boy with eels, Comacchio.

figures showed that recruitment was down to about 120,000 of the million glass eels necessary to maintain the equilibrium. To make up the difference the Cooperative began buying glass eels captured near the mouth of the River Severn at Gloucester in the West of England, and live-hauling them in trucks to Lough Neagh. Unfortunately, recruitment has fallen so low in recent years that making up the difference is too expensive, and there is no way the Cooperative can afford to introduce enough glass eels to balance supply and demand.

The Cooperative's factory and offices are in Toome, on the banks of the Bann, close to the Lough. When the autumn migration begins, and the fat, protein-rich silver eels come downriver toward the North Sea, they are at their tastiest, and they are the most prized. In the river is a stone weir, an ancient method of fishing for eels in which converging walls slowly herd them onto a trap as they descend the river in autumn. The walls narrow to a small space, below which lie nets that can be winched up, and on dark, cold and moonless nights in Toome, those nets

A fisherman with eels in a net, Comacchio.

An eel trap, or *ahinaki*, made from vine, mid-19th century, New Zealand.

come up out of the water brimming with silver eels. In the autumn of 1964 nearly 450,000 kg (1 million lb) were captured. Forty years later, in 2006, the catch was under 45,000 kg (100,000 lb) and falling.[32]

Draw a ragged diagonal line right across Europe, north to south, and things are no better in Lake Comacchio on Italy's Adriatic coast, some 50 miles south of Venice, a vast sprawling

Eel canning at Comacchio, 1927.

wetland that includes a huge lagoon of brackish water at the mouth of the Po River. A system of weirs called *lavoriero*, with v-shaped walls built of reeds woven tight and stretched between wooden posts, was first mentioned in a written document in 1494, but it is believed to date much farther back. Comacchio was controlled for centuries by an aristocratic family of north-eastern Italy named Este. The eel fishermen's lives were as close to slavery as skin to bone, and history does not record a single visit of an Este family member to the flat, wet, cold, malarial shores of Comacchio. They did scrupulously send their agents every year to collect high tributes in eels. In 1500 the worth of an entire year's eels from Comacchio, some 45,000 gold *escudos*, is said to have paid for the construction of the family's fabulous Palazzo dei Diamanti in Ferrara.

In 1598 Pope Clement VIII wrested control of the region from the Estes. He was, apparently, an eel lover and was known to come to Comacchio and enjoy a hearty repast. It was at Comacchio, in the eighteenth century, that Mondini would discover the female reproductive organs of the eel, and eel specialists have long made the place a centre of their investigations. In the first part of the twentieth century, on moonless, stormy nights during the autumn migration, the eels were often so thick coming into the traps that bonfires were lit along the shore to slow them down.[33]

In 1714 over 907,000 kg (2 million lb) of eels were taken in the traps, a figure matched in 1914.[34] Only another twenty years after that, however, the numbers had fallen below 90,700 kg (200,000 lb), never to rise again. By 2006 the catch was down to around 907 kg (2,000 lb) a year and falling annually. Lake Comacchio is 12,000 hectares of water and wetlands, a lagoon the size of Milan. Fifty years ago, before Italian authorities began to dredge it for development purposes, there were nearly 60,000 hectares. The wetlands have been reduced by 80 per cent since Benito Mussolini's rule. These days the entire year's eel production no longer provides any significant contribution to the economy. Comacchio's eels do not even come close to providing the nearly 50,000 lb of eel served over the two weekends in October when the town holds its annual eel festival.

Eel fisheries all across Europe are experiencing the same declines, and the drop in numbers is felt in every European Union country with a coastline. In each of these places an economy exists that is built around an eel fishery. In some of them it is the capture of glass eels that generates incomes, and in others it is the adult eel that is prized. In both cases the resource is drying up, disappearing, growing scarcer year by year.

What usually happens to glass eels and elvers when they are caught is that they are sold live to Chinese aquaculture operations, which will raise them on fish farms to sell as adults to the Japanese. In Japan the eels will wind up as *kabayaki*, a favourite dish in which pieces of eel are butterflied, skewered, marinated in a thick soy sauce and steamed or grilled. More than 90 per cent of the eel eaten each year in Japan is prepared as *kabayaki*. The Japanese demand is too large to be met by the native *Anguilla japonica* eels entering fresh water from the Pacific Ocean, and over the past couple of decades, in years when the glass eel catch in the Pacific has been low, Chinese and Japanese businessmen have bought glass eels in both Europe and the USA. While the Japanese hold that the European and American eels have less flavour than their native species, they will eat them rather than not eat eel at all. A glass eel captured as it enters an American or European river and freighted on a plane to China is never going to reproduce, but it is going to generate considerable economic activity.

In years when the Japanese and Chinese are paying top dollar, a lot of money can be made during the autumn, as the glass eels move into the rivers. The years of 1996 and 1997 saw a drastic shortfall of *Anguilla japonica* glass eels coming into Korean, Chinese and Japanese rivers from the Pacific Ocean, and prices for them went sky-high in Europe and the USA. In New Jersey, during the moonless, windy, cold and ill-tempered nights when the glass eels like to move upriver, representatives of Japanese eel farms stationed themselves on the same banks with their pockets full of cash. They were paying as much as $500 per lb (0.5 kg), tax free, and just a few pounds made for an extremely nice night's work. Disputes over riverbank rights occasionally broke out and there were evenings when shots were fired. Then the prices fell and the glass eels were left alone, once again, to try their luck in the rivers.[35]

A more organized glass eel commerce exists in Europe. In fact, according to EU figures, at least 400,000 lb (181,450 kg) of European glass eels have gone to Asia each year, with at least a thousand of them in a pound.[36] That represented about half the annual catch. The other half, except for a very few that wind up being eaten locally, go to European grow-out farms, where they are kept until reaching table size, then often sold on to China or Japan as adults.

In Spain and England elvers are held in high esteem as food. The English scramble them up with eggs, and the Spaniards like to flash fry theirs in a dash of olive oil with a mildly piquant pepper. However, because of their value on the international aquaculture market they are tremendously expensive when bought locally and no longer form part of a standard diet. In Spain's Basque region, in the first half of the twentieth century people netted glass eels and fed them to the pigs, but by 2000 a plate of them in a Bilbao restaurant could cost £40.

Most people in the USA would rather skip a meal than eat an adult eel, while most European diners will tuck into one with gusto. The few adult eels fished commercially in the USA are shipped to other countries by air, or sold as bait to striped bass fishermen. Adult eels captured in European waters are more likely to wind up on local tables. In Europe they are much appreciated as food. The manner in which they are prepared and consumed varies widely from country to country, as we shall see in the following chapters, but they are eaten all across Europe, and form one of the oldest foods in the cuisine of Euro-Caucasians who live anywhere near eel waters.

The International Council for the Exploration of the Sea (ICES) estimates that 25,000 people in Europe currently fish for eels commercially, making it the largest inland fishery in Europe.[37] To what degree fishing pressure has contributed to

F. Cooke, eel and pie shop in Broadway Market, Hackney, London.

the decline of European eels is a hotly debated topic. It is also one of the few variables in the eel equation that is amenable to human legislative controls and EU lawmakers have recognized the gravity of the population decline by imposing stricter regulations on both the adult and the glass eel fisheries, even while they wait for science to explain it. Of course, those representatives of countries that fished for adult eel and left glass eels alone were in favour of the strictest regulations being applied to baby eel dealers, while those whose business consisted of buying and selling glass eels insisted that it was escapement back to the Sargasso by sexually mature eels that had to be regulated. As it happened, everyone took a hit. By the end of 2008 EU countries must have eel management plans in place. At least 40 per cent of the eels in each nation's rivers must be able to make an unimpeded journey to the sea.

It was also ruled that, by the year 2013, glass eel fishermen must be setting aside 60 per cent of their catch 'for restocking of European inland waters so as to increase escapement of adult eel to the sea'. Well, 2013 was still fairly far in the future. Glass eels are worth a lot of money and that 60 per cent seemed harsh, even to the lawmakers, so they qualified it: 'In case of significant difference between the price of glass eel destined for restocking and the price of those marketed for other uses, the percentage required to be set aside for restocking will be temporarily reduced in order to counter the price discrepancies.'[38]

A sufficient number of loopholes and postponeable deadlines, combined with a bureaucratic tendency toward commissions, reports and constituent pressure, makes it unlikely that much can be done by legislative bodies to reverse the eel decline, if the population is really in free fall. However, in Europe they have decided to try. Contrary to the conclusions drawn by the USFWS about the American eel, the Europeans have decided to treat eels as an endangered species and their declining numbers as a sign that the species is 'outside safe biological limits'. In June 2007 *Anguilla anguilla* was accorded protection status under the Convention on International Trades in Endangered Species (CITES), which allows authorities to severely limit the number caught, as well as to take steps to protect its habitat. Enforcement was scheduled to begin in 2009 but no one was certain what new rules would be enforced and how. It is not easy to accurately estimate fish captures and in 2007 there were still countries with no counting mechanism in place.

Perhaps drastic and concerted action now will turn the eel's population around, as has happened with other species, such as the striped bass along the northeast coast of the USA. A well-designed emergency programme certainly will not do any harm and might do a lot of good. On the other hand, if the decline in glass eel recruitment is caused by something happening in the

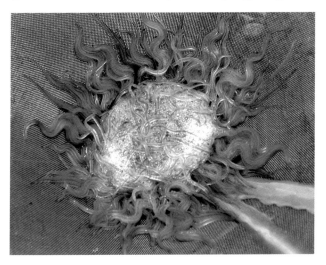

Elver fishing, Charente, France.

Sargasso, all human effort will be in vain. Eel biology may well be beyond the limits of human influence.

Eels are subject to the depredations of various parasites and diseases and these may be contributing to recent declines. For instance, the European eel is known to have gone through periods of high mortality caused by the nematode *Anguillicola crassus*, which affects the swim bladder. Possibly the eel population is under attack by a disease we have not identified. Or perhaps the decline is part of a cycle we have yet to perceive and one day soon, for no apparent reason, the glass eels may resume arriving at our rivers in massive wriggling walls of baby eels, and the silver eels may again make their migrations to the sea in such numbers that bonfires will need to be lit on dark and nasty autumn nights to slow them down. The current decline may simply be a low point in a cyclical process rather than a descent towards extinction.

Not everyone believes that eel apocalypse is upon us, although the most insistent voices asserting that what we are seeing is a natural cycle and not a catastrophe are those who depend on the fish to make a living. They have some scientific evidence to bolster their arguments. A 2006 study carried out in the USA seems to indicate that while glass eel recruitment fluctuated from year to year, it was not in a continuous decline. Glass eel counts were made in Beaufort Inlet, North Carolina, and Little Egg Inlet, New Jersey, over the course of fifteen years and they showed a wide range of recruitment.[39]

That has not happened in Europe. Glass eel catches plummeted between 1994 and 2004 in all the countries where they are still fished commercially: France, Spain, England, Ireland and Portugal. During that same decade small commercial glass eel fisheries that existed in Italy and the Netherlands disappeared entirely. Is the eel in danger of following suit and vanishing from our world? Would it make any difference if it did? Most people would probably never note the absence of fresh-water eels from the world's rivers, lakes, ponds, streams and creeks, but it might be instructive to consider what we will be losing if they do disappear. Eels nourished our forebears and we owe them protection for doing so. The history of humanity and eels is a long and noble one that bears remembering and celebrating.

3 Classical Eel

He stood at night when eels
Moved through the grass like hatched fears
Seamus Heaney, 'A Lough Neagh Sequence' (1969)[1]

The unknowns surrounding the eel's past and eel's future, the deep mysteries of the eel question, have never, throughout history, impeded the average citizen from tucking into a dish of eels. Human appreciation of eels has never depended on our understanding the how, where or why of eel biology, but rather on their full rich flavour and easy availability. One of the many things that European and American adult eels have in common is that the meat of both species tastes nearly the same – a rich, pure fish flavour that can be delectably prepared in a great many ways. They taste good to human beings. We may not know much about them but most people who think about eels are not interested in observing them, but in eating them. 'Fear death,' wrote the Greek comic poet Philaeterus around the end of the fourth century BC, 'for when you're dead you cannot then eat eels'.[2]

Long before the Greeks began recording in words what they saw in the world around them, people were eating eels. In fact, it is safe to assume that in many parts of the ancient world prehistoric populations counted on eels as a primary source of sustenance during certain seasons of the year. Wall paintings in French caves from Palaeolithic times represent eels, and the trash middens left behind by the Palaeolithic population of caves at Baoussé-Roussé contain eel bones, according to Gwenn-Aël Bolloré.[3] In central France, a carved stone cylinder was found in a cave near the Vézère River, featuring a human, two horses and an eel.[4] 'Remains of eels from prehistoric sites in Europe are by no means widespread or abundant, though sufficient bones were found at Ertebölte in Jutland and [at] Hemmor, Gottland to indicate that they were caught in substantial numbers at least during the Stone Age in the Baltic area', wrote J. C. Wilcocks in 1865.[5]

In Northern Ireland, where the River Bann empties into the same sea, one of the world's prime eeling grounds, archaeological evidence found close to the river reveals quantities of fish bones and pieces of wood thought to be part of ancient eel traps. In 1951 a harpoon worked out of wood was discovered at Toome and dated to 5725 BC. Today in Toome, almost eight thousand years later, autumn still means a silver eel harvest. These are the eels of Lough Neagh descending the Bann. The Lough's yellow eels are fished year round, but the flavourful silvers are only caught in the autumn when the sexually mature silver eels come down the Bann river, swimming by night to reach the sea and begin the voyage back to the Sargasso. Thousands of years ago people must have waited as eagerly for

An ancient Egyptian 'eel coffin', a sheath for a mummified eel, the animal sacred to the god Aton.

Eel trap on a beach near Norsminde, Denmark.

the eels to begin migrating as they do today. While they may not have had a written language, it is certain that prehistoric peoples had observed the eel closely enough to know that it was at its fattest, tastiest and most numerous in the fall, and the middens – the garbage heaps – of prehistoric settlements in these places show us that this was so. They yield a high percentage of eel bones, and it is likely that people followed them down the Bann as they descended, eating and perhaps smoking and preserving them along the way.

The first appearance of eels in Western writing does not relate how to eat them, however, so much as what they will eat, in this case human flesh. Homer, in the eighth century BC, distinguished them from all other fish, and stressed one of their least attractive qualities: that they are not hesitant to feed on recently dead flesh. In the *Iliad*, when Achilles has fought and killed Asterpaíos on the banks of a sea-going river, the epic poet says:

> With this he pulled from the bank's overhang
> his bronze-shot spear, and having torn the life
> out of the body, left it there, to lie
> in sand, where the dark water lapped at it.
> Then eels and fish attended to the body,
> picking and nibbling kidney fat away.[6]

The great Greek traveller and chronicler Herodotus recorded in around 450 BC that in Egypt the eel was treated as a minor deity, with a cult of its own. Alexandre Dumas, writing in France more than two thousand years later, noted in his *Grand Dictionnaire de Cuisine* that the Egyptians kept them in ponds where acolytes fed them daily on cheese and the entrails of animals.[7] The contemporary French writer Gwenn-Aël Bolloré described the cult in her book on eels, claiming that it used the eel as a representation of the emergence of the newly born, sacred sun from the waters.[8]

Rather than regard the eel as a minor god, the Greeks accorded it food-of-the-gods status. Numerous references in Greek writing attest to the position of respect it was accorded at the table. In fact, writes the comic playwright Antiphanes, his compatriots in the fourth century BC paid even higher tribute to

A wood engraving of an eel from Dumas' *Grand Dictionnaire de Cuisine* (Paris, 1873).

the eel than the Egyptians. 'They say that the Egyptians are clever in that they rank the eel equal to a god, but in reality here it is held in esteem and value far higher than the gods, for *them* we can propitiate with a prayer or two, while to get even a smell of an Eel at Athens we have to spend twelve *drachmae* or more!'[9] While eel would eventually become a popular food among the Athenians, it was a fish with a price that reserved it for the well-to-do. David Badham, in *Prose Halieutics*, writes of one Philiteus who held that to be rich and not to have tasted eel should be numbered among the serious misfortunes of life.[10]

The Greeks had other ways of paying tribute to eels, although some did attribute a divine origin to them. The poet and parodist Mataro, more or less a contemporary of Aristotle, wrote of the eel lying in Zeus's embrace. It was Zeus who caused the rain to fall, and eel propagation was widely believed to be connected to rainwater. Other writers called them the king of fish. The eels from the huge Lake Copais in Boetia were considered the best. The people of Boetia had a bad reputation among the Athenians for being coarse, uneducated people, but they were recognized and regarded for their eels. In his play *Lysistrata*, Aristophanes' title character calls for the destruction of Boetia and all its inhabitants but qualifies her anger by adding, 'except the eels'.[11] Aristophanes seems to have had a weakness for the eels of Lake Copais. In another of his plays, *The Archanians*, a character receives news that someone has brought him 50 eels from the lake, and he exclaims, 'O my sweetest, my long-awaited desire'.

Another community that exalted the eel to nearly deific heights were the Sybarites of the Greek community of Sybaris on Sicily, a community that thrived from about 720 BC until it was wiped out by war in 510 BC. The Sybarites were known for their love of luxurious and lazy living and for their abhorrence of anything resembling hard work. In *Fishing from the Earliest Times* William Radcliffe reminds his readers that it was the Sybarites who 'felt they had broken their bones if they saw another person digging, and suffered not a cock in the whole country, lest he should mar their slumber'. They were, he tells us, so devoted to eating eels that they passed legislation exempting eel sellers from taxes and tributes as an incentive to keep a steady supply of them at reasonable prices.[12]

A common love of eels was even enough to halt a war, according to Waverly Root in *Food*. He recounts that when the Carthaginians came to conquer Syracuse, the two opposing armies set up camp outside the city. For supper the day before the battle, soldiers from both sides went out to hunt eels in the marshes. Bound by a common love of eel, the men began to fraternize and by morning the Carthaginians decided to pack up and go home rather than kill their fellow anguilophiles.[13]

Not all Greeks were so quick to sing the praises of eels. Some Greek medical professionals held that they had harmful effects, particularly when consumed in large quantities. In fact, the man regarded as the father of modern medicine, Hippocrates, warned that eating eels could be harmful to people with certain health conditions, as did Seneca and Galen, according to Badham. The Roman writer Pliny the Elder, however, seems to have hedged his bets in the second century. He asserted that eels are bad for the throat and can make people lose their voices, but then went on to say, 'This is all the harm they do'. On the other hand, conceded Pliny, 'Singular are they holden to bee for to cleanse the humours, either cholericke or phlegaticke, likewise to cure the infirmities of the spleen'.[14]

Perhaps, Badham speculated, the real danger to health from eating eels was simply eating too many of them, goaded on by gluttony and pure pleasure, and this explained their bad reputation among medical practitioners. 'We may here howeverer suggest that possibly an indiscreet use of this too luscious food, and not any bad quality in the fish, deserved this blame.'[15] Those who like to eat eels have often liked to eat them to excess. While the Romans appear to have favoured the marine conger eel more than the freshwater European eel, its consumption was not unknown to them. The second-century satirist Juvenal painted the crassness of a host who served eel to his guests:

> Now comes the dish for thy repast decreed
> A snake-like eel of that unwholesome breed
> Which fattens where Cloaca's torrents pour,
> And sports in Tiber's flood, his native shore;
> Or midst the drains that in Suburra flow,
> Swims the foul streams, which fill the crypts below.[16]

In the first century AD the Roman epicure Marcus Gavius Apicius wrote that 6,000 eels were served at feasts celebrating the victories of Julius Caesar and that they were supplied from the famous fish ponds of one Gaius Hirrius. Apicius was one of the most famous epicures of all time. He inherited a tremendous fortune, which he spent as freely as he could on the good life. It is said that when he was reduced to being merely well off, instead of tremendously wealthy, he became obsessed with the idea that his fortune would dwindle away until he could no longer lay out the sort of table he enjoyed, and committed suicide rather than accept a life under such straitened circumstances.

He was also the author of the first cookbook, *De Re Coquinaria*, or at least the volume bears his name, as it is generally thought that it was compiled for him rather than by him. The scant regard paid by the Romans to freshwater eels is evident in that the book contains only one entry for freshwater eel, and it gives the ingredients for two sauces to serve over an eel, although there is no explanation for how to cook it. The 'Ius In Anguillem' recipe reads: 'Eel will be made more palatable, by a sauce which uses pepper, celery seed, lovage, anise, lyrian sumack, figdate wine, honey, vinegar, broth, oil, and mustard. Cook it.' This is followed by a second eel sauce recipe containing dry mint, rue berries, hard yolks, pepper, lovage, mead, vinegar broth and oil.[17]

A century later the amazing Greek poet and natural historian Oppianus of Cilicia wrote his five-volume *Halieuticks of the Nature of Fishes*, consisting of 3,506 hexameters, according to Radcliffe, an encyclopaedic poetry in which he uses the first two volumes to describe the natural history of 153 different species in the waters of his world. The last three volumes are devoted to fishing for those species. In the natural history verses he has a go at the eel question, and while his conclusions are as erroneous as Aristotle's 500 years earlier, his verse is evocative. His contention was that mating eels produced a fertile slime.

Strange the Formation of the Eely Race,
That know no sex, yet love the close Embrace.
Their folded Lengths they round each other twine,
Twist am'rous Knots, and Slimy Bodies join;
Till the close Strife brings off a lively Juice,
The Seed that must the wriggling Kind produce.
Regardless they their future offspring leave,
But porous Sands the Spumy Drops receive.
That genial Bed impregnates all the Heap,
And little eellets soon begin to creep.
Half-Fish, Half-Slime they try their doubtful Strength,
And slowly trail along their wormy length.[18]

Oppianus' father is said to have been exiled from Cilicia to Malta when he failed to go and pay his respects to Lucius Verus, a visiting dignitary who was close to the emperor Marcus Aurelius. Oppianus went to Malta with his father, but after the offended Verus died he went to Rome for a visit, bringing his verses with him. He presented them to Marcus Aurelius, who was so impressed that he pardoned Oppianus' father and gave the young poet a gold piece for each of the hexameters. Little it served him, as he died at 30 years old.

Not much hard evidence of eel eating has turned up from Europe's so-called Dark Ages. What is certain is that it was a popular dish. With meat prohibited on numerous days of the years in the Church calendar, flesh of the flavourful fishes was an ordinary substitute on many a table. And why not? Eels were plentiful and cheap, if not free, for the easy fishing, and they are a rich and flavourful fish. Tom Fort's *The Book of Eels* reports an archaeological dig in the lakeside town of Oldenburg in Schleswig-Holstein that revealed more than half the fish eaten between 650 and 900 were eels.[19]

Eel is popular in Germany, and Germans have eaten them copiously since prehistoric times. Arturo Bellini, from Comacchio, studied the *lavoriero* and the history of eel fishing among his fellow Comacchiese, then undertook a research trip to the Baltic sea in 1902, where he spent a year studying the eel fishery along the German coast and in the rivers of north-west Germany. Bellini built Comacchio's only palace, which today houses a museum and the town library. On a shelf at the library is the manuscript Bellini wrote about his German sojourn. In it, he recorded the antiquity of German dependence on the eel. '[F]or the North Germans, the eel was an inexhaustible supply of food . . . so, for example, in the Middle Ages eel constituted one of their principal and most appreciated sources of nutrition

Eel fishing, a 15th-century manuscript illumination.

Lamprete comple fri + hui id˜ minozus tennen trudicans gramquille
Hic sunnis derienns sup petras manriena impremena et nitri nicut Nor
sto deblet hude vemo noz in salmdie + pipe Laud thuma thiorum fleci
Conemus mach calie + str Inneibs axtupno et efface septet˜ ga mele dicten

Lampreten · seind laile vnnd faist in anndern grad. doch nit so feicht als die Lel. Die in fließenden
rauhen Bachen gefanngen seind die besten · Sie macheud haist vnnd nennd wol · schaden dem bloden
faisten Magen · berais mit saltz vnnd essici macen pflegenaltsig gestlict siegen mer den warme
fangen im Herpst vnnd Sommer · vnnd kalten lannden · dann da werden sie bald verderbet ·

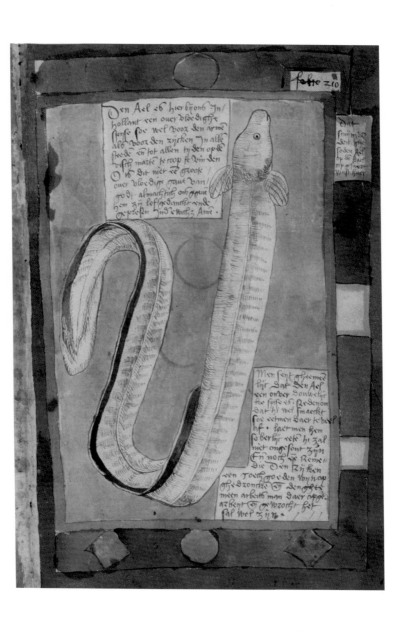

and it was so common in those provinces that servants stipulated in their contracts that their employers would not feed them eel more than twice a week.'[20]

Eels were so numerous that sometimes it wasn't even necessary to fish for them; they could simply be gathered up out of the fields at night when they slithered ashore to come and steal the crops, or so some people believed. Real proof has never been presented that they deliberately come ashore to pilfer crops, but an eel can do pretty well on dry land. Its slime will keep its skin moist enough to stay alive for a couple of days,[21] if it finds leaves to hide under or mud to burrow in when the sun is up. Eels do willingly cross dry land to go between one body of water and another, and it is not surprising that over the years people who live near eel waters might have seen one on dry land. But no record exists of someone actually watching an eel eat a plant on shore. Just its presence out of the water is probably enough to engender the idea that it climbs ashore to search for food. The first mention in print of the phenomenon came in Albertus Magnus's thirteenth-century *Book of Animals*, where he wrote about eels leaving their ponds at night: 'The eel also comes out of the water in the night-time into the fields where he can find pease, beans, or lentils.'[22] After feasting in the farmers' fields, assured the monk, the eels would slither back to the water before sunrise.

In 1686 the Oxford chemistry professor and naturalist Robert Plot published *The Natural History of Staffordshire*. In it he writes about Staffordshire eels crossing dry land:

> But for breeding and living, there is no fish so wonderfull amongst all the scaly or shelly kinds, as there is amongst the smooth ones, *viz.* the common eele . . . which will sometimes take journeys *in arido*, passing over land from Lakes and Pooles they do not like to others they

An eel illustration in Adriaen Coenen's *The Fish Book* (1577–81).

like better: by this means many times stocking waters of themselves, which were not so before . . .

. . . for most certain it is that Eeles are such night walkers, as was suggested above, having been actually catch't in the very fact near Bilston creeping over the meddows like so many snakes from one ditch to another, by Mr Mosely, who seriously told me that they not only did it for bettering their station but as he apprehend, also for catching snails in April and May, the best time of the year for them.[23]

In a rather fanciful book published in 1834, quite popular in its day, called *Gleanings in Natural History*, Edward Jesse, the Royal Surveyor, purported to have heard a remarkable tale from a reliable and sober fisherman who lived in Kingston-upon-Thames in Surrey. The fisherman told Jesse that he brought a freshly

Frans Snyders, *Fish Market*, 1625, oil on canvas.

caught batch of eels home in a pot one evening and left it in his garden. 'On visiting it the next morning,' writes Jesse, 'all the eels were gone, and he concluded that they had been stolen. At least a month afterwards, however, he found the eels hidden amongst the turf . . . in his garden, all perfectly healthy and in good condition. This was in the Autumn when there was much dew on the grass. The eels had probably fed on earth worms.'[24]

As recently as 1882 a correspondent wrote to the magazine *Land and Water*:

Last week I saw eel fishing going on in the County Wexford marl holes [large, open, abandoned excavations for marl clay filled with water]. Many of these holes are at great distances from the streams and river, and have no connection with them, so that the eels must go over land to get to them, and I learn from the people in the neighbourhood that some of the largest eels they get are caught in the grass in summer after rain.[25]

Regardless of whether eels really do spend time on dry land, people have pursued them where they live to capture them, and put them on their tables. Eel dishes are included in the first recipe books on both sides of the English Channel. In France eel recipes figure prominently in the collection *Le Menagier de Paris*, 'a treatise on moral and domestic economy' written by an anonymous older Parisian to instruct his much younger wife in her duties and responsibilities, published in 1394. Its topics range from how to make ink to how to keep their bed flea-free, and a lot of attention is paid to the wife's culinary duties. For hostesses, the book has 24 full menus, some for meat days and some not, with recipes for preparing their dishes. And, in those days, a full menu meant what it said. The first one, for instance,

was six courses, comprising 31 dishes, and including a 'soringue' of eels. This was prepared by skinning and cutting up the eels, frying them with onions and parsley, then boiling them with ginger, cinnamon, cloves and saffron and adding a purée of toasted breads, verjuice, wine and vinegar.[26]

Even a pope was not immune to the temptation offered by the rich flesh of eels. Martin IV's weakness for both eels and wine was legend, and Dante Alighieri, in *The Divine Comedy*, described the pope's punishment for his gluttony: 'That [man] behind him, his face more sunken than any other, once fathered Holy Church. Of Tours his line; and here in the long fast he expiates Bolsena's eels and the Vernaccia wine.'[27] Dante's tomb is in Ravenna, hard by the River Po's marshlands that surround Comacchio, and he no doubt knew whereof he spoke when it came to eels. Comacchio's eels have a reputation for excellent flavour stretching back many centuries. Every autumn men would go out into the marshland and spend months eating and sleeping in rough quarters, tending the eel traps, using the system and tools handed down for centuries. The nights were wet and cold and their quarters were rudimentary stone houses far out in the marsh, where their lives were hard ones, according to Tom Fort. 'They slept in their damp clothes on mud floors, fed on eel heads and those unappetising slabs of baked maize flour called *polenta*, their provisions strung up from the beams to keep them from the rats which scuttled among them as they lay.'[28]

On the River Kennet in mid-Victorian England: *The Eel Traps on Kennet – After a Shower*, by Henry John Boddington (1811–65), oil on canvas.

The traps were emptied into huge round wicker baskets called *bolaghe*, which were sunk nearly to their tops, allowing water to circulate through the basket and keep the eels alive, not allowing them to wriggle out. At the end of a long night's work a line of these floating baskets would be hauled behind a boat to Comacchio and their contents would be delivered to the factory. There a seated man in a leather apron with a hatchet and a chopping block in front of him took them up one by one and cut their heads off. The bodies were then spitted, each spiked through twice in an S-form, and when the spits were full they were carried to a rack under a huge brick chimney, where flush-faced women turned them over the heat of roaring fires. Once cooked, they were sealed inside barrels, packed and preserved in a spiced vinegar

An eel trapper at work.

Weirs in the lagoon of Valli di Ferrara at Comacchio.

and shipped to the big cities. Another way in which Comacchio's catch was marketed was a system of live-haul transport, in which the eels were held in long wooden containers shaped like covered dug-out canoes, with small open spaces in the joinery, allowing water to circulate. These were towed behind another boat to Venice, or to Naples, where Comacchio's eels were prized.

Eel was cooked in numerous ways in Italy, depending on the region. It was an important dish among the seven fish dishes served on Christmas Eve as the *pranza di natale*. A recipe for eel pie was included in *De Honesta Voluptate et Valetudine* ('On Honourable Pleasure and Health'), published in 1474 by Bartolomeo de Sacchi di Piadena, known to his contemporaries as Platina. The recipe's instructions make it evident that cooking an eel was a serious endeavour, and among the ingredients needed to prepare the eel for the pie were suet, mint, parsley, pine nuts, raisins, ginger, cinnamon, pepper, cloves, almonds and saffron.

In France, the skewer was foresworn in favour of simmering eels in such dishes as a *matelote*. It is the most traditional French way to eat eel but it is by no means a standard preparation. One book describes it as eel chunks simmered in white wine or red vinegar with herbs and onions and maybe mushrooms, while another author raves over a *matelote* in which the eel was stewed for two hours in red wine with Malaga grapes and prunes from Agen. In addition to the various *matelotes*, eel was also prepared in France as a pâté, grilled, smoked, stewed and gelled. French cookbooks have been full of eel recipes since the fourteenth century. Not only cookbooks, according to Gwenn-Aël Bollaré in *La Saga de L'Anguille*, which contains some tasty recipes itself:

> It is the literature of the Middle Ages that most fully celebrates the eel. This fish that not only intrigued and hid its secrets, but which also nourished in a season when the peasants were vulnerable to the cruel wind, and at the mercy of whoever came along; when the rigours of winter wiped out the stores, when the animals die of the cold and when warlords have taken everything left, how can you not dream of a good matelote or a succulent paté of fish, which the warlords are, and rightly so, incapable of capturing for themselves?[29]

As early as the mid-thirteenth century cooked food was available on the streets of Paris. Guillaume de Villeneuve described the cries of the hawkers pitching their products in the street, and their offerings included waffles, hot mashed beans, cheeses, hot pancakes, boiled and roasted beef, mutton, pork, lamb, kid, pigeon, capon and goose, along with hot pasties filled with chopped pork, chicken or eel.

A taste for eel knows no borders. That eels were prized by the English is certain. The eighth-century monk the Venerable Bede recorded that King Ine, who promulgated the earliest laws of Wessex and reigned there from 688 to 725, stipulated that among the annual rent for a small landholder would be ten geese, twenty hens, ten cheeses, a full amber of butter, five salmon, twenty pounds of fodder and a hundred eels.[30]

It was one of the primary links in our food chain. For all the differences between Italian, French and English cuisines, people on both sides of the Channel depended on eel for sustenance. The streets of London also had their fast-food outlets, including one around 1170 close by the River Thames that offered all sorts of prepared foods to suit the tastes and pockets of everyone from a poor person to a member of the landed gentry, according to

Grilling eels at Comacchio's eel festival.

Menu advertising
eels in
Comacchio.

Marinated eel for
sale.

Martha Carlin in *Food and Eating in Medieval Europe*. In fact,
eels are mentioned in writing as early as the Domesday Book of
1086, where it is recorded that Evesham Abbey had an eel fishery on the River Severn that yielded as many as 2,000 eels at a
time. Many monasteries had ponds in their grounds where fish
could be held as part of the food stores.

The first English cookbook, *The Form of Cury*, is thought to
have been compiled somewhere between 1370 and 1400. In it is
a recipe for eel pie:

> Stew it in almond milk and verjuice [the ultra-acidic juice
> of the immature grape]. Mix almond milk with the stew.
> Pick out bones and clean fish, save middle piece whole of
> eels and grind the rest small. Add powder, sugar and salt

A canal street
in Comacchio.

Eels on spit,
Comacchio.

and grated bread; and fluff the eels therewith, there where the bones were mix the other part of the other mixture and the milk together and colour it with sandalwood. Make a crust in a dish and bake it therein and serve it forth.[31]

In a poem by Piers of Fulham, thought to have been written around 1420, the poet decries the frivolous waste practiced by those who kill young eels for their livers, while discarding the rest of the fish. Eel pasties may have been plentiful on the streets of France and England, and prepared food generally available in cooks' shops, but that does not mean they were always healthy. As much can be deduced from the fact that in Coventry the Town Hall took the trouble in 1421 to forbid cooks to buy dead pike or eels to bake into pies or pasties. In Chaucer's *Canterbury Tales* the question of hygiene in food shops is also raised.

'That gentleman appears to be having quite an altercation with those eels!' This cartoon by E. Four shows the copy in the Tuileries Gardens, Paris, of the famous Greek statue that actually depicts the doomed Trojan priest Laocoon and his two sons being killed by poisonous snakes.

One of the earliest English cookbooks, John Russell's *Boke of Nurture*, perhaps written as early as 1445, included a recipe for roast eel. Russell's was one of the first books of a genre that is still popular: the revelations of a servant or an employee about the life of his or her employer. In this case Russell revealed what dishes he prepared to nourish his master, Humphrey, Duke of Gloucester. Books revealing the secrets of the kitchens of the rich and famous never fell out of favour. In 1588 a man named Robert May, whose father was a chef and sent him to be trained as a young man in the kitchens of Paris, wrote a book about his lifetime as a chef to the nobility, and included sixteen different eel recipes in his book, *The Acomplisht Cook, or the Art and Mystery of Cookery*. In 1655 an even more impressive tell-all book

Jan van Kessel (1654–1708), *Still Life*, oil on copper.

Jean-Honoré
Fragonard, 'Eel
pâté', c. 1775, an
illustration for a
story by Jean de
La Fontaine.

of recipes was published, directly from the heart of the Queen's kitchen. Its author was identified only as 'W.M., one of her late servants'. The book was titled *The Queen's Closet Opened*, and claimed to be a direct transcription of 'true copies of her majesties own Receipt Books'.

To prepare eels for a queen was not something done quickly, or simply. For instance, W.M. provides instructions 'To Sauce Eels':

> Take two or three great Eels, rub them in salt, draw out the guts, wash them cleane, cut them athwart on both sides sound deep, and cut them againe crosse way, then cut them thorow in such pieces as you think fit, and put them into a Dish with a pint of wine vinegar, and a handful of salt, have a kettle over the fire with fair water, and a bundle of sweet herbes, two or three great Onyons, some Mace a few Cloves, you must let that lie in wine, vinegar and salt, and put them into the boyling Liquir, there let

Discussing dinner
in Victorian times.

94

the boyle, according to cookery, when enough take, take
out the Eeles, and drain them from the Liquor, when they
are cold take a pint of white-Wine, boyle it up with Saffron
to colour the Wine, then take out some of the Liquor, or
put it in an earthen pan, take out the Onyons and all the
herbs, onely let the Cloves and Mace remain, you must
beat the Saffron to powder or else it will not colour.[32]

While the nobility savoured their eels in sophisticated sauces,
the poor fried or stewed or boiled or broiled them, served them
jellied or served them grilled, but served them they did on many
a supper table across Europe. The Thames itself was home to
eels, although it did not produce anywhere near the numbers
needed to satisfy the appetites and market for them in London.
The Fens of East Anglia were one of the medieval world's richest
eel grounds. The Severn, in western England, had huge walls of
glass eels moving upriver in the spring and adult eels making for
the sea in the fall. However, the English eel fisheries basically
supplied local markets. Eels must be prepared freshly killed,
because they go off quickly after dying. It was not easy to transport live eels to London's clamouring hordes, even if more than
enough could be caught to satisfy local demand.

The Dutch, on the other hand, already had a well-oiled international eel shipping industry up and running. In the early
Middle Ages, according to Tom Fort in his *Book of Eels*, they were
dealing in live eels along the North Sea coasts, from Holland to
the Baltic states. Dutch ships, towing the same sorts of partially
sunk, live-haul wooden crafts being used in Comacchio, bought
and sold eels. By 1472 the Dutch were buying eels to bring to
London and sell at Billingsgate. The city's demand was such that
there were not enough English eels to fill it. Dutch schooners
brought thousands of pounds at a time. In 1472 King Edward iv

granted a licence to an Amsterdam eel dealer to do so. The international eel trade prospered, and the numbers were so large that the price of eels remained at affordable levels on even the most meagre of daily budgets. *Anguilla anguilla* fed Londoners from the queen to the street sweepers, bringing protein and calories to the masses throughout the Middle Ages.

4 Puritans and Victorians

From the eels they formed their food in chief,
And eels were called the Derryfield beef;
It was often said that their only care.
And their only wish and their only prayer,
For the present world and the world to come,
was a string of eels and a jug of rum.
Anonymous 18th-century New Hampshire poet[1]

In September 1620 a group of townsfolk, religious separatists from England, set sail for the New World on the *Mayflower*, determined to found a colony that would adhere to their interpretation of the Holy Word. That they were thinking less than clearly is evident from the time they chose to begin their voyage. A well-designed journey to New England began in late winter or early spring, timed for an arrival in early summer; to make landfall in the autumn was to guarantee hardship. But how could they have known? No one had settled there before.

The *Mayflower* pilgrims seem to have been mainly composed of people who had bought food from others at a market all of their lives, and who were unprepared to wrest nourishment from the natural world around them, particularly not in the midst of a New England winter. Their hunting and fishing skills were amateurish at best, and it was too late in the year to begin planting. The community was kept busy with sickness, death and mourning. Half of them died during the winter, and the rest lived on meagre rations and in deep dread of the savages they believed were lurking in the vast woods around them.

It was one of those savages who saved the lives of the remaining pilgrims, when he came out of the woods with a companion and approached them in April 1621. He did it even though in the early 1600s he had been captured and put to work like a slave

A swarm of eels in a holding tank.

on board an English ship-owner's vessels. Tisquantum, known in Euro-American history books as Squanto, was fully acquainted with the treachery of white men. By the time he was returned to New England shores by his captors, in 1619, his whole tribe had died out, extinguished by influenza introduced by the English. Yet he saved the survivors at the Plymouth settlement from their own ignorance and taught them how to live from the land and water around them. The first thing he showed them was how the Native American people had caught eels from time immemorial by wading into the river, treading them up and spearing them. This was a food that the Pilgrims could relate to, something familiar that they knew how to prepare. Many of them were from the Fens region of eastern England, where eels were common fare.

An ancient diet of eels was a taste the European settlers shared with the Native Americans. Archaeologists have excavated a site on Kejimkujik Lake in Nova Scotia, where they believe pre-historic people lived during the eel season, where the remains of eels were reported to be about 5,000 years old.[2] The mighty St Lawrence river delivered large numbers of eels to inland water-ways, and they fed untold numbers of people. Among the multi-tudinous tribes of Native Americans living with access to rivers or streams or creeks where eels made their homes, many different means were used to capture them. The same methods were used by prehistoric Europeans and humans everywhere to put eels on the table – spears, traps and weirs – although their form and con-struction varied depending on local conditions. In what is now Quebec the native fishermen used all three methods.

The Native American use of eel is commented on by many of the early observers of the New World. As eel fed the *Mayflower* pilgrims, so it fed the original Americans down through North American prehistory. From Florida to Quebec there is evidence of eel consumption by Native Americans. As early as 1535 the first French explorer of Canada, Jacques Cartier, was recording the importance of smoked eels in help-ing local tribes provide sustenance to their families during the long, harsh winters. The first of the Franciscan missionaries, Father Pierre Biard, who came to Acadia in 1611 to convert the heathen, was impressed by the orderly and functioning society he found among the native Mi'kmaq tribe. He was also impressed by the abundance of the natural world around them. The eels were 'good and fat', he wrote, adding that they were so thick in the water that a person could not put a hand in without touching one. These words were echoed by another early French traveller to the New World, Pierre Boucher, who wrote back to Paris: 'There are eels, larger and better than in France and in such quantities as cannot be conceived without being seen'.[3]

Father Biard's Franciscan mission eventually failed, and he left Acadia. Not long thereafter the Jesuits attempted to carry the Word further into Canada. Gabriel Sagard-Théodat, in the Jesuit's history of the early missionary voyages, deemed that eels saved many Native Americans from hunger. 'Eel in the proper season is an invaluable article to our Montagnais', he wrote in 1634 from Quebec:

> I have admired the extreme abundance of the fish in some rivers of our Canada, where every year uncountable hundreds are caught. They come just in time, for, were it not for this succour, one would be greatly embarrassed, more especially in some months of the year; the savages and members of our orders use them as meat sent by Heaven for their relief and solace.[4]

Differences were found among the ways that Native Americans consumed their eels, although the sum of the ways in which they were cooked was the same as that of Europeans. The Algonquins smoked them, like the Scandinavians, Germans and Dutch. In other places they split and grilled them, spatchcocked, it was called. The Iroquois were reported to spit their eels on green branches and broil them over the flames, just as they did in Comacchio under the huge chimneys, or to use them in a thick soup like a French *matelote*. 'Their food is generally boiled maize, or Indian corn, mixed with kidney beans, or sometimes without', wrote Daniel Gookin in his 1677 *Historical Account of the Indians*. 'Also they frequently boil in this pottage, fish and flesh of all sorts, either new taken or dried, as shad, eels, alewives, or a kind of herring . . . These they cut in pieces, bones and all, and boil them in the aforesaid pottage.'[5]

Not all the Europeans who ventured early on to the New World were as disappointed in their hopes and expectations as the *Mayflower* pilgrims. Many wrote home of their astonishment at the riches of the game and fish in this fresh, new world. John Josselyn was a contemporary of the Plymouth settlement. His father was an English knight who fell on hard times and had to sell off the ancestral manse. John's oldest brother, Henry, having few prospects left in the Old World, set sail for the New about the same time the *Mayflower* arrived at Plymouth. He made it to what is now Maine, where he laid claim to a vast expanse of land. He was a Royalist through and through, loyal to king and country. The *Mayflower* band detested him. His younger brother, John, spent ten years with him, and later published in England his account, *Two Voyages To New England*. 'I never eat better eals in no part of the world that I have been in, than are here', he wrote about the bounty of Maine's rivers. 'They that have no mind or leasure to take them, may buy of an Indian half a dozen silver bellied Eals as big as those we usually give 8 pence or 12 pence for at London, for three pence.'[6]

The anthropologist Frank Speck found the Penobscot tribe in Maine still consuming them in quantity as late as 1910. 'Eels are split open, the backbones being taken out and saved to put into corn soup, and the carcasses hung up on a frame like the smoking rack to dry or to be smoked. In winter they are frozen. Boiled over again they make excellent soup.'[7]

Some early chroniclers of New World tastes were not as exaggerated in their praise, but all agreed that eels were plentiful and perfectly edible. In 1634 William Wood wrote in *New England's Prospect* that that Indians in Massachusetts around the marshlands near the ocean took quantities of eels in pots. '[S]ome take a bushell in a night in this manner, eating as many as they neede of for the present, and salt up the rest against winter. These eels are not so luscious a taste as they be in England . . . but they are both wholesome for the body, and delightfull for the taste.'[8]

By this time the Plymouth community had settled in and eel had become a staple on their table. Smoked meat was what brought many settlers through the long hard winters, and smoked eel was a standard component of winter's stores. Despite the memories of the hardships he had suffered through that first year in Plymouth, Edward Winslow, one of the *Mayflower* band's leaders, could write to a friend in England describing the abundance of the New World: 'Fresh cod, in the summer, is but coarse meate with us . . . In September we can take a Hogshead of Eeles a night, with small labour, and can dig them out of their beds, all Winter.'[9]

One of the early ways cooks prepared fresh eel was as eel stifle. Potatoes and onions are layered with eel in a pot, with a little flour between the layers. Salt pork and pork fat were put on top and water added nearly to cover. It was cooked until the meat was firm and tender and the potatoes were done. An eel stifle is still occasionally served on Martha's Vineyard, and instructions for it still turn up in collections of New England recipes. It was also called an eel smother, sometimes corrupted into 'smudder', as in this notice from the *Mystic Press* in December 1876: 'The eelers appeared on the [Mystic] river last week after a long absence, and the lovers of eel "smudder" may now gratify their gustatory longings for that savory potpourri.'[10]

Even after the Europeans had settled North America in numbers and organized it into a familiar, functioning and reliable society, where people could choose what they wanted to eat rather than having to eat what was at hand, eel remained a favourite. Up and down the East Coast, but particularly in New

England, they were highly regarded. The first North American cookbook was written by Amelia Simmons and published in 1796 in Hartford, Connecticut. However, cookbooks published in England during the 1700s found a receptive audience of readers in the New World. Cookbooks by English authors like Hannah Glasse or Susannah Carter were widely read, and they all had eel recipes. They were reprinted in New England and sold well. Glasse's *The Art of Cookery* first appeared in 1747; Carter's was published in Boston in 1772 with illustrations by Paul Revere. It included a recipe for broiled eel, which, according to Keith Stavely and Kathleen Fitzgerald in *America's Founding Foods*, was just a rewrite of an earlier Hannah Glasse recipe. Glasse's book had a section called 'For a Fast Dinner, a Number of good Dishes, which you may make use of for a Table at any other Time.' Herein were nine eel recipes, including eel soup, eel pie, stewed eel, potted eel and how to 'pitchcock' an eel. Her book was so popular in England that it went through twenty editions in the eighteenth century.[11]

Dancing for eels in 19th-century America.

Unsurprisingly, when Amelia Simmons published that first Yankee cookbook, it contained a recipe for fried eels, which recommended that they be so fresh when cooked that they jump when they are dropped in a frying pan, as chunks of a recently killed eel will appear to do. An eel has a lot of life in the pan. One New Englander who was not a great admirer of *Anguilla rostrata* was Henry David Thoreau. In 1849 he described an eel from the Merrimac River: 'a slimy, squirming creature, informed of mud, still squirming in the pan, speared and hooked up with various success'.[12]

The first bestselling American cookbook was published in 1824. Its author was Mary Randolph, a 62-year-old widow of a tobacco planter, who took up keeping a boarding-house in Richmond, Virginia, after her husband died. Her father was Thomas Jefferson's foster-brother. Her cookbook had three recipes for eels and went through six editions. Modesty had initially impelled her to publish the book without her name on it, but she was listed on subsequent editions.[13]

Meanwhile in England, and all over Europe, the eel market had continued growing. It was important enough to become a political issue, to generate laws, rules and regulations. As early as 1412 London authorities were intervening in the eel trade, with the Lord Mayor decreeing that the price of eels was to be determined strictly by its weight and nothing else, and that a fair price per pound would be set by the Mayor himself. In the early 1600s the British Parliament enacted stiff protectionist measures that barred many kinds of imports. Among them were cod and live eels, the mainstays of London's fish consumption. It cut off the traditional market of Dutch ships that loaded up with eels in Denmark and brought them to England and up the Thames to sell at Billingsgate, the city's huge fish market.

It was not many decades before eels were in short supply and the price for them had risen substantially. During the same time, the Fens, the eastern England wetlands famous for copious quantities of eels, were drained and canalized, resulting in a precipitous decline in the number of eels caught. By the late 1600s high market demand, combined with the destruction of habitat in the Fens, had created a shortage of domestic eels. A similar problem existed with cod – not enough of them were being caught to serve the market. Not only was it a popular fish in domestic cuisine, it was carried aboard ships in its cured form to provide food over a long voyage at sea, and these were the years in which the English were sailing the world's seas. As cod and eel grew scarcer and more expensive, sentiment turned against the duties on fish from foreign waters.

In 1680, faced with these shortages, Parliament passed an Act allowing the importation of live eels and cod. The reasons for rescinding the prohibition as it regarded eels were enumerated in the legislation, chief among them being that 'there is not the hundredth part sufficient taken in England to supply the Kingdom'. The legislation also evoked the image of Dutch eel ships at anchor in the Thames, calling it a sight that Londoners had seen 'time out of mind, as will appear by all the Ancient Mapps of the City of London, where you will find the Eel-Ships always figured out in the River of Thames, lying at anchor'. Furthermore, the Act went on, 'Live eels are esteemed (as in truth they are) most Excellent Food (The Price being set by The Right Honourable the Lord Mayor of London) are bought and sold at very reasonable rates.'

The legislation was passed and in no time the huge, wooden planked, two-masted Dutch schooners were again anchored off the Billingsgate market wharves. Eventually a royal decree gave them the exclusive right to supply eels to Billingsgate.[14] The

Billingsgate fish market at the end of the 19th century.

decree stipulated that at least one ship must always be anchored at the market with eels for sale, thereby guaranteeing a steady supply to the city in return for the franchise. The schooners were the long-distance trucks of their time, live-haul eel sellers, bringing live fish from Holland to England. The interior of the ships was fitted with a pool of water sided with wooden slats that allowed water to circulate, while keeping the eels trapped. These live-haul ships were called *schuyts*, and could hold well over 100 tonnes of eels, according to George Dodd in *The Food of London*. Each morning before dawn Billingsgate's eel wholesalers were rowed out to the ships to go aboard and do business. They would descend into the watery hold and buy their day's eels. The vessel stayed until the pool was empty, then turned for home and a new load.

In his four-volume masterwork *London Labour and the London Poor*, Henry Mayhew, the great chronicler of Victorian London's working poor, described business on a Dutch eel boat anchored out from Billingsgate:

When a skiff load of purchasers arrives, the master Dutchman takes his hands from his pockets, lays down his pipe, and seizing a sort of long-handled landing-net scoops from the tank a lot of eels. The purchasers examine them, and try to beat down the price. 'You call them eels do you?' said a man with his bag ready opened. 'Yeas,' answered the Dutchman without any show of indignation. 'Certainly there is a few among them,' continued the customer; and after a little more of this kind of chaffering the bargain is struck.[15]

Once in the market, the eels were wholesaled to fishmongers throughout the city as well as to those agents buying in bulk for elsewhere. After those deals had been transacted, there were still eels to be sold to costermongers. (In the seventeenth, eighteenth and nineteenth centuries London's streets were full of peddlers and pushcart vendors, and these people were called costermongers, or costers.) Mayhew reported in 1851 that by his calculations 9,797,760 eels were sold annually at Billingsgate, and that one-fourth of that number, or almost 2.5 million, were sold to costermongers, which would have been some 185,000 kilograms (408,000 lb) of eels. In addition to those who sold eels, which they generally served either stewed or in pies, costers offered a wide variety of ready-to-eat fish and seafood, including cockles, mussels, boiled whelks, pickled salmon, smoked herring, oysters, lobsters and crabs.

The costermongers mainly tended to live in London's East End. They made only the most precarious of livings from their street vending, and were pressed on all sides. The police harassed them because they did not have licences, but they did not prohibit them entirely because without costermongers poor people would have had no source of daily sustenance on the streets. Generally the costers rented their barrows with the small portable ovens set in them on a daily basis, and bought the stock they thought they could sell by day's end. The rent on the cart was due, come hell or high water, at the end of the day. If for some reason sales were bad a coster could well finish the day losing money. And it was a long day. They had to be at Billingsgate or other markets to buy their provisions before first light, and they stayed out until they sold what they had or gave up.

Not all the meals served up by costermongers met basic hygiene standards. The chopped meat that went into minced meat pies, for instance, was often of dubious provenance, and it is said that occasionally dogs or cats were used, to say nothing of those parts of a cow that were not good for anything else. Better to stick with eel, many consumers decided, although truth to tell that was not entirely safe, either. Dead eels could be bought cheaper than live at Billingsgate, and mixed in with the spiced stewed eels minced up into pie filling at a saving to the coster. Among pie men, a mix of 50 per cent dead eels was considered more than fair to the customer, according to what the eel pie vendors told Henry Mayhew in 1851. He recounted one conversation: "'And after all,' said a street fish dealer to me, 'I don't know why dead eels should be objected to; the aristocracy don't object to them. Nearly all fish is dead before it's cooked, and why not eels? Why not eat them when they're sweet, if they're ever so dead, just as you eat fresh herrings?'"

In the seventeenth century restaurants for the average worker did not exist, but a wide menu was available from the costermongers' carts. By the mid-eighteenth century, as eating places began appear and gain popularity, two prominent eel pie houses were opened. One of them was on Twickenham Island just off the city's southwest shore on the Thames. In 1737 an inn was built

A puffin with a mouthful of sand eels.

amidst the island's willow trees, and the owner gained fame for his delicious eel pies, so much so that the island became better known as Eel Pie Island. By the 1800s it was a popular recreation to take a brief boat ride to it, stopping off for an eel pie lunch and a stroll before heading back to the city. In 1839 Charles Dickens wrote of such an excursion in *Nicholas Nickleby*: 'Unto the Eel-Pie Island at Twickenham, there to make merry upon a cold collation, bottled beer, shrub, and shrimps, and to dance in the open air to the music of a locomotive band.'[16]

Eel pie is an old English favourite, stretching all the way back to that recipe for it in *The Form of Cury*, from 1400. In London the first eating establishment dedicated to eel pie was recorded in 1844, in Kelly's *Trades Directory*. It belonged to one Henry Blanchard and sold various pies, including meat, eel and fruit, for a penny apiece. Live eels, mashed potatoes and peas were also sold.[17] By 1860, according to Jim Smith in his book, *Pie 'n' Mash: A Guide To London's Traditional Eating Houses*, London was home to about twenty eel pie restaurants, over thirty by the

Mark Salt of the National Anguilla Club with a 6lb 3oz eel caught the previous night.

end of the 1870s and over a hundred by the turn of the century.[18] As these places grew in popularity, demand plummeted for eels bought on the street from costermongers, and the cries of 'Eels O! Eels O! Alive! Alive O!' dwindled into silence.

During the twentieth century the eel pie houses developed into 'pie and mash' shops, and by the first decade of the twenty-first century over 70 of these curious little restaurants were spread across London, the direct descendants of the costers with their barrows. They often have a nineteenth-century decor with tiled walls and long wooden tables that diners share. A five-pound note buys a big plate heaped with mashed potatoes and stewed eels, all covered in a parsley-and-flour gravy with a paste-like consistency, called 'liquor'. The customer tops off the plate with plain or hot vinegar to taste. Eel is a rich, tasty fish, and no one leaves hungry. The lines at lunchtime are often out the door in these places, which also offer meat pies instead of eels to accompany the potatoes. Manze's Eel and Pie House, located alongside the Chapel Street market, served about 250 portions of eel a week in 2007, according to owner Tim Nicholls, along with more than a ton of potatoes.

Pie and mash shops may still have a steady clientele, but the eel-eating habits of Londoners, and the English in general, have changed drastically since the Second World War. Jellied eel, for instance, was a perennial favourite, sold at fishmongers everywhere. Today, apart from at pie and mash shops, it is almost impossible to find, although a stall or two at Billingsgate will have them on hand. Jellied eel does not appear on the shelves of local supermarkets, and neither does any kind of eel at all. Even less trace of a culinary appreciation of eels is found in the USA, where they began to drop off the menu after the Civil War ended in 1865. While Americans of Italian descent continued to eat eels, by 1920 they were no longer considered fit for the table by most people, despite their status as a 'founding food'. Cookbooks are an excellent way to track what people are eating.

How to skin an eel.

Cookbooks published in the USA since 1950 rarely contain even one recipe for eel. In England, while its consumption has diminished, the eel still gets its share of respect. As recently as 1973 an illustrious food writer confessed in her *Jane Grigson's Fish Book*:

> I love eel. Sometimes I think it is my favourite fish. It is delicate, but rich; it falls neatly from the bone; grilled to golden brown and flecked with dark crustiness from a charcoal fire, it makes the best of all picnic food; stewed in red wine, cushioned with onions and mushrooms, bordered with triangles of fresh bread, it is the meal for cold nights in autumn; smoked and cut into elegant fillets, it starts a wedding feast or a Christmas Eve dinner with style and confidence.[19]

This sort of praise is not likely to be heard in the USA from food book writers or anyone else. Eels have disappeared from the inventory of edible fish, and recipes for preparing them are virtually nonexistent. Japanese restaurants have introduced a new form of eating eel, *kabayaki*, to those cities with enough people to support one, but this new taste has not done much to restore eel to the Yankee menu. It's a shame, because eel is such a tasty fish, but it's a fact. For the eel, of course, it is better this way. Although glass eel recruitment is generally down in America, as in Europe, there is much less pressure on existing stocks of adults.

5 Sniggling

O to have been brought up on bays, creeks, lagoons,
   or along the coast!
O to continue and be employ'd there all my life!
O the briny and damp smell – the shore – the salt weeds
   exposed at low water,
The work of fishermen – the work of the eel fisher and
   clam fisher.
Walt Whitman, 'A Song of Joys'[1]

Because they have disappeared from the national larder, in
Yankee waters eels are pretty much left alone to live out their
lives in whatever water they choose, and eventually to travel,
unmolested, back down-river to the sea. A handful of people
along the East Coast trap eels, which they sell to wholesalers,
who pack the eels in dry ice and put them on a plane for deliv-
ery as air freight to a European buyer. Another handful sell
young eels to striped bass fishermen along the Atlantic coastline. A young, foot-long eel is irresistible bait to a striped bass.
Generally, however, when eels are caught in North American
waters it is by accident, and most people who find an eel on the
end of their fishing lines are not happy about it.

Almost everyone in this situation is inclined to return the eel
back into whatever body of water it came out of as soon as possible, but that all too often turns out to be not so soon as they
wish, because the distance between the desire to throw an eel
back in the water and the necessary prerequisite of getting the
eel off the hook can be considerable. The first problem is that
eels are virtually impossible to grasp, and the second is that the
eel immediately twists its body and becomes intertwined with
the line. For some reason, people often think that using a newspaper to hold one will make the task easier, but they find out in

Eels for sale
in Chinatown,
New York.

114

short order that the newspaper only tears into small slimy bits that stick to the hands as the eel slithers through them. With a towel wrapped around an eel, a person can grasp it tightly enough to remove a hook, but for those who do not have one to hand an eel can ruin a perfectly good day's fishing.

That attitude is as senseless as the refusal to eat eel. It is not only a delicious fish when landed, but it puts up a strong fight. Let an eel get its tail wrapped around a submerged log or other obstruction, and pulling it loose can be virtually impossible, with all but the strongest lines parting before the eel lets go of its grip. A metre-long eel can provide plenty of fishing excitement, but in the USA people fail to take advantage of it. Not so in the UK, where eel fishing clubs still thrive, and competition for the big eels is fierce. The current record holder's prize catch was an 11 lb 2 oz (5 kg) eel taken in 1978 at Kingfisher Lake in Hampshire.[2] The secret to catching really big eels, counsel the experts, is to find isolated bodies of water where eels have become trapped; unable to return to the Sargasso when they reached sexual maturity, they simply carry on living the life of a freshwater eel, feeding until they reach much larger than normal size. A big eel is an old eel, and they can live a long, long time, although they no doubt stop growing somewhere along the line. The oldest eel on record seems to have been a Swedish eel which lived to an estimated age of 85, spending her last years in a museum.[3] Another example is an albino eel kept in an aquarium in Trocadero, Spain, from 1913 to 1946.[4]

Over the millennia a lot of advice has been given by experts on how to catch eels of all sizes, and they have been fished for with a remarkably wide and imaginative range of gear. Take, for example, the method recommended by the Greek naturalist Oppianus, around AD 170, in Book XIV of his *Halieuticks of the Nature of Fishes*. The fisherman first obtains a long intestine from

A mouthful of eel while out netting in Gava, Spain.

a freshly slaughtered sheep. Into this he inserts a hollow reed and lowers the entrails into the water. A tug on the intestine signals that an eel has bitten it. Acting rapidly, the fisherman puts his end of the reed in his mouth and blows through it as mightily as possible. The air descends the intestine and enters the eel's mouth and its windpipe, and it cannot breathe.[5] Shortly there-after, the Roman Claudius Aelianus wrote of the same method in his mixture of fact and fable, *De Natura Animalium*: 'As the Eel can neither breathe nor detach its teeth which are fixed in the intestine, it is suffocated and drawn up . . . Now this is a daily occurrence, and many are the Eels caught by many a fisherman.'[6]

Despite the antiquity of these rather bizarre instructions, hollow reeds were by no means the first equipment used to fish for eels. That distinction belongs to the human hand. Treading up eels in the mud and catching them barehanded was no doubt practised long before other fishing technologies were invented. One of the first refinements on this most primitive fishing technique of lunge-and-grab was the spear, confirmed by such finds as the 7,000-year-old remains uncovered in Northern Ireland, by the River Bann.[7]

The spear continued to be a favourite means of catching eel for home and local consumption. A speared eel was often too

A scene from Milton's *Paradise Lost*: the creation of the fish and the birds, an engraving by Gustave Doré, 1870.

damaged an animal to offer at a public fish market, but was perfectly fine to bring home for supper or sell to neighbours. In 1843, for instance, one J. C. Bellamy published *Housekeeper's Guide to the Fish Market*, advising British homemakers on how to shop for fish. He advised keeping an eye out for eels during the cold months, when they were speared 'in great numbers' while they lay in the mud.[8] In 1863 G. C. Davies recorded that in the Norfolk Broads an eel spear was called an eel 'pick'. 'Eel picking is an art in which some men attain considerable skill. The eel picker in his little punt is a common object on the flats.'[9]

In the USA spearing eels was also practised since time immemorial. The Jesuit father Paul Le Jeune was one of the earliest missionaries to live among Native Americans. He spent ten years among the Montagnais in what is now Quebec and recorded his observations and experiences while trying to convert them. The Indians who fished for freshwater eels did so with spears, he wrote to his superiors in Paris. He described the harpoons used by the Montagnais as being tridents, the middle tine of which was fixed iron (and bone before iron was available), but the outer two were curved and gave way when an eel was struck, rising above the writhing body and closing around it in such a way as to keep it fast.

> This fishing with the harpoon is ordinarily done only during the night: two savages sit in a canoe, one behind who steers and paddles, and the other ahead, seeking by the light of a bark torch, attached to the prow of the craft, his prey with his eyes, while gently moving along the bank of this great river. Perceiving an eel, he darts his harpoon without losing hold of it, pierces the eel . . . then throws it into his canoe. Some will catch three hundred, and many more, in a single night, but very few at other times.[10]

As recently as 1915, those who could handle a spear well were able to earn a living during certain months of the year practising their art in New York and New England. Those who fished in the rivers feeding Raritan Bay between Staten Island, New York, and New Jersey were spearing 68 kilograms (150 lb) a day during winters when the fishing was good, and regularly earning four dollars for a day's work. As winter approached and the water temperature fell, the eels sought the muddy bottom in which they would wait out the season. They would lie at the bottom, covered by an inch or two of stiff mud. When the ice thickened enough to walk on, the fishermen would go to their favourite spots, chop holes in the ice and jab their 5.5 metre (18 foot) long spears through them. If they got an eel, they would bring it up and shake it off the spear on to the ice, where it would freeze and could be collected at day's end where it had landed. The only problem was that seagulls had to be constantly shooed away from snatching the frozen eels.[11]

Northern Ireland's River Bann has also yielded the remains of yet another ancient method of fishing: the weir. Because yellow eels do not tend to wander far, weirs are not the best way of capturing them. But the strategy works well with silver eels, as they head downstream towards the ocean. They are moving fast and in masses, and they can be herded by subtly directing their course. The silver eel is considered the tastiest of eels; it is the moment in the animal's life when it has the most stored fat and protein. A 4,000-year-old line of wooden stakes, connected by wickerwork, has been found close to Toomebridge in Northern Ireland. The structure was a weir, with brush mounted on it to herd migrating silver eels into traps. The same brush and branch walls were being used in Comacchio to direct eels to the *lavorieros* in the Middle Ages, just as the native Americans living by the great rivers that emptied into the Atlantic built their brush and branch weirs, and the stone weirs in the River Bann still serve to drive the eels into the nets of the Lough Neagh Fishermen's Cooperative at Toomebridge. Father Paul Le Jeune was much impressed by the weirs that the Montagnais built. He recorded how they constructed walls of stones in the river to direct the eels into traps. On dark, stormy nights they could gather hundreds in this fashion. The Onondaga of New York built weirs along certain stretches of their rivers and allotted them to the chiefs of various bands to exploit.

These two devices – the spear and the weir – function best when fishing for eels in different stages of their lives. The spear will catch mainly yellow eels, burrowed into their homes, or close by them. The same is true of a trap, laid out nightly during the many months of the year when the eel is feeding. The trap is another ancient fishing technique. The first ones were made with wild, strong, fibrous reeds, woven together into a basket with the same basic design as all the other eel pots, eel traps and eel boxes that would follow: a funnel leading into a chamber from which the eel cannot figure out how to return. If the traps are placed at the narrow end of a weir it is not necessary even to bait them.

Some Native American methods of eel fishing were more localized. Up to the twentieth century the Penobscot tribe of Maine was using an ancient method to fish for them. Anthropologist Frank Speck observed it around 1910. They crushed large quantities of berries from the poke bush with the roots of Indian turnip and spread it across the surface of the river. Soon stunned eels began floating on the surface, where they lay helpless and dying. The Indians gathered them up and brought them to shore where they were skinned, salted, dried and, finally, smoked.[12]

For most people, however, the preferred way to catch a yellow eel for the supper table has been the same as any other fish – with a line and some bait. The English call this kind of eel fishing

'sniggling', derived from the word 'snig', meaning a small eel, and first recorded in 1614 according to the *Oxford English Dictionary*. The *OED* also lists a definition from 1775: 'to fish for eels by putting bait to the holes in which they conceal themselves'.

The oldest recorded advice for eel anglers in England was written by a fisherwoman. 'A Treatyse of Fysshynge with an Angle', by Dame Juliana Berners, was published in *The Boke of Saint Albans* in 1496. Berners was born in the late fourteenth century, and is thought to have been prioress at Sopwell nunnery near St Albans, and to have been a great devotee of hunting, falconry and fishing. She was no fan of eels, but deigned to include them in her treatise, in recognition, no doubt, that the tastes of large numbers of her readers did not agree with hers. 'The eel is an unhealthy fish', she wrote, 'a ravener and devourer of fish's broods, and as for the pike he is also a devourer of fish. I rate these below all others to angle. You will find the eel in holes at the bottom of the water, and he is blue-black. Sink your hook until it is within a foot of the hole, and your bait must be a large earthworm or minnow.'[13]

England's most famous how-to-fish book is *The Compleat Angler* by Izaak Walton, first published in 1653. In contrast to Dame Juliana he had the highest respect for eels, counting them as an excellent catch ('It is agreed by most men, that the Eel is a most daintie fish'), and he devoted a number of pages to propagating mistakes about their biology. In addition he extolled the pleasure of fishing for them: 'in a warm day in Summer I have taken many a good Eel by snigling and have been much pleased with that sport.' Izaak Walton was in agreement with Dame Juliana about one thing: earthworms are an excellent bait. He added that bits of chicken or fish guts could also serve. Once the hook was baited:

Put in your bait, but leasurely, and as far as you may conveniently: and it is scarce to be doubted, but if there be an

Eel traps and fishing nets along the Dutch coast.

Eel bucks were used to trap eels in the Thames.

Clot of worms for use in fishing.

Eel within the sight of it, the Eel will bite instantly, and as certainly gorge it: and you need not doubt to have him if you pull him not out of the hole too quickly, but pull him out by degrees, for he lying folded double in his hole, will with the help of his tail break all, unless you give him time to be wearied with pulling, and so get him out by degrees, not pulling too hard.[14]

About four hundred fishermen in Toomebridge, Northern Ireland, earn their livelihoods catching eels in Lough Neagh with worms in one of Europe's most important adult eel fisheries. The Lough Neagh eel is considered by many gourmands across Europe to constitute the tastiest example of *Anguilla anguilla*. The fishermen at Lough Neagh, a 16-mile-long lake and one of the five largest in Europe, say the eels that live there taste so good because a major part of the fish's diet is the Lough Neagh fly, a gauzy-winged insect related to the mayfly. The Lough Neagh fishermen catch their eels between 1 May, when the water warms and the eels begin feeding, and mid-November. They use long lines, sinking 1,200 baited hooks, and they spend a couple of hours each morning digging up the worms to bait them with from their private worm patches.

Worms work well as bait, as they do with most fish, but eel bait comes in plenty of other forms. A survey was done in England between 1974 and 1982 of 321 persons who landed eels weighing more than 1.8 kg or 4 lb. A 4 lb eel is a big eel. Among those surveyed, 186 caught their eels on earthworms, 96 on dead bait, fourteen on maggots, seven on live bait, eight on cubes of lunch meat, four on swan mussels, two on a bit of cheese and one each on a kernel of sweet corn, a crab, a trout fly and a crayfish.[15]

Some remarkable variations on the standard hook-and-worm strategy have been elaborated over the centuries, not the

A. Demarest,
*Family of
Fishermen*, 1890,
oil on canvas.

least weird of which is 'bobbing', which has been practised for
centuries in Europe. Recorded instances of its use stretch back
to at least the early 1600s, and the first reference to bobbing listed in the *OED* for the US was in 1815. Bobbing consists of using a
stout needle to thread a large clump of worms with cloth or
yarn, and lowering the whole to the bottom, at night. An eel will
bite the ball of worms and its teeth will become entangled in the
fabric so that it can be brought directly up to the boat or on to

the bank. Bobbing crossed the Atlantic at some point. It is referred to in a book published in 1866 called *Athletic Sports for Boys*, in which the anonymous author explains how to prepare the clump of worms and writes: 'Bobbing for eels is a very amusing night sport.' For those boys who followed his suggestions and found themselves with an eel onshore, or in a boat, the book also offers some eminently practical advice: 'The way to grasp an eel . . . is to place the second finger on one side of him, and the first and third on the other, about an inch and a half from his neck. Then by pressing the fingers together he cannot move'.[16]

In Raritan Bay yellow eels were caught by bobbing through the first part of the twentieth century, with a group of dedicated fishermen doing so in March and April of each year. Clyde McKenzie Jr records in his book about Raritan Bay's fisheries that each person fished two bobs, and each bob had about 30 worms on it and was about the size of a fish. It was common for an individual to catch 45 kilograms (100 lb) of eels a night, but many of them would be undersized young eels, which got tossed back in the water.[17]

Another peculiar method of eel angling was recorded by Cyrus Adler, a self-described urban naturalist, in New York City.

Lonfin eels feeding, Mount Bruce, Wairarapa, New Zealand

In a note published in *Underwater Naturalist*, he recounted his experience walking through lower Manhattan one morning in the 1960s, about 2 a.m.:

Midwinter Eel-fishing on the River Neva in Russia, 1881, engraving.

I came across a man sitting on a wooden box next to an open manhole on Water Street. This spot is near the East River, one of many low areas built on filled land. The man sat smoking a pipe and held a cord in his right hand . . . As I watched I saw him draw up the cord from the sewer hole – it was attached to an umbrella handle. He grabbed the handle and pulled it up further; water squished out of the umbrella. Then he tipped over the umbrella and emptied a mess of wiggling eels into the crate next to him. He took a puff on his pipe and lowered his fishing gear down into the sewer hole by its handle.[18]

Adler's tale might initially appear far-fetched, but a review of the literature proves that eels are as at home in the water pipes of cities as they are in the mud of their rivers. Gratings were placed across the entrances to London's main water pipes to keep Thames eels from moving into them. During the twentieth century the *New York Times* carried a number of reports of eels found blocking water pipes from the Bronx to Brooklyn and in Manhattan. In fact reports of eel blocking water pipes have come from such far-flung locales as Dartmouth, Nova Scotia, and Wanganui, New Zealand, according to E. W. Gudger, writing in *The American Midland Naturalist* in 1950. As early as 1883 numerous eels were found in the water pipes of New Bedford, Massachusetts.[19]

In addition to an individual angler sniggling for a meal of eels, people fish for them commercially. For this, traps and fyke nets get added to the list of ways used to catch them. In Europe eel remains the most commercially important inland fishery in many places, but catch figures are generally declining, whether from a scarcity of eels or a reduced number of people fishing for them is not clear. In 1950 the United Nations Food and Agriculture Organization (FAO) reported a total landing of 13,188 tonnes of yellow and silver eels. By 2001 the figure was down to 1,685 tonnes, and a number of countries that had previously supported thriving eel fisheries were no longer reporting any commercial catch.[20] Even with shrinking numbers some 25,000 Europeans were still fishing for eels, a total that includes people who fish for and sell them in each of the three stages of their lives: glass eels, yellow eels and silver eels. Almost all the yellow and silver eels are consumed in Europe. Yellow eels are the simplest to catch, available at least half the year, and requiring only simple gear like long lines or traps. They also fetch the lowest prices. Silver eels, because they are at their fattest and tastiest, are only fished in the late autumn months when

Patrick Johnson fishing for eels on Lough Neagh, Northern Ireland, 2001.

they migrate downriver to the ocean. Because they are taken en masse, the gear required is heavy and more complicated. These are mostly bought by high-end markets in Europe.

It is safe to say that the eels in the world could indefinitely sustain the European market without posing any danger to their numbers, but the driving forces behind the world's eel market are China and Japan. Eel is prepared as *kabayaki* and eaten in great quantities in the dish called *unadon*, grilled on a skewer and served in a bowl over rice. The Japanese appetite for eels is insatiable and is rising steadily. In 1986 they ate 11 million kg (24.2 million lb), and by 2005 that number had quadrupled to nearly 91 million kg (200 million lb), about 60 per cent of which was imported from China, already grilled.[21] There were some 67 plants in China buying eels and turning them into *kabayaki* to be exported to Japan, and each of the plants was producing 3,000–4,000 tonnes a year. How much this market pressure has contributed to the decline of the European eel is hard to quantify but it has certainly played a large role, as it has in the dwindling numbers of so many other species ranging from blue-fin tuna to octopus.

Across the ocean from Europe, along the Atlantic coast in states from South Carolina to New England, only a handful of people still fish commercially for yellow eels. The season will last for two or three months in the spring and two or three months more each autumn. The traps they use are rectangular, made of galvanized wire. They have a canvas funnel at one end, leading into the trap, and the other end is latched so it can be opened and the eels poured out. The traps are baited with recently killed crabs or trash fish, and set on the bottoms of rivers and estuaries. The people who fish traps during eel season tend to be fairly reclusive, and they often reside outside of town: far outside, and many of them live by the dictum, 'Mind your own business and I'll mind mine.'

Different types of eels, including the common Moray (both top) and the European eel (bottom left).

130

Generally, they are not given to a great deal of faith in, or admiration for, their fellow human beings. They are people who fish for whatever is in season, and when eels are feeding that's what they fish for. Other times of the year they may set gill nets for whatever comes along, or go crabbing, or clamming or shrimping. They catch eels in baited wire traps, holding each night's take for a week or two in an underwater cage until a live-haul truck comes by and picks them up. The driver writes a check for the eels, then they are packed in boxes with dry ice and taken to an airport where they will be put on a plane to Europe. A shipment of eels to Italy, for instance, might consist of 2,700 kg (6,000 lb) or so. Fewer and fewer people are fishing for them, and landings have steadily declined, although the dollar's weakness against the euro during the first decade of the twenty-first century helped keep it going.

In the United States commercial landings for eels declined from a high of just over 1.8 million kg (4 million lb) in 1982 to under 0.5 million kg (1 million lb) in 2004, according to a report of the Atlantic States Marine Fisheries Commission (ASMFC).[22] There is also a market for young eels in the 15–23 centimetre (6–9 inch) long category for sale to striped bass fishermen along the Atlantic coast. It is an even more informal market than that for adult eels, operative during striped bass season, and it is impossible even to estimate the numbers of eels sold for this purpose, although in spring and autumn most bait shops in striped bass territories will have some on hand. Fishing with young eels is not for the squeamish. There is something about meeting the eyes of a young, live eel while putting a hook through its lips that is distinctly uncomfortable. Still, the possibility of coming back from a day's fishing with a 14 kg (30 lb) striped bass seems to overcome those qualms for a lot of people. The self-described last person in Rhode Island still to be making a full-time living from eels told me in 2001, 'I used to catch big quantities of adults, and

Larvae caught in a single two-hour haul by Johannes Schmidt in the Western Atlantic in the early 20th century.

did well at it for many years. I used to catch 1,000 lb a day. Now, a good day might be 200 lb. Fortunately, as the number of big eels declined, [the government] opened up striper fishing and the demand for bait eels grew.'[23]

Glass eel fisheries in the United States are pretty much a thing of the past. The bonanza nights of the mid-1990s, when buyers for the Asian grow-out farms came to the riverbanks with

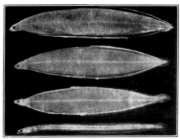

1. AMERICAN EEL (ANGUILLA ROSTRATA). METAMORPHOSIS OF LARVAE. THE TOP SPECIMEN IS A FULL-GROWN LARVAE BEFORE METAMORPHOSIS, THE LOWER ONE AN ELVER. GULF STREAM AREA OFF THE ATLANTIC COAST OF THE UNITED STATES
Natural size. (From Johs. Schmidt, l. c. 1916)

2. EUROPEAN EEL (ANGUILLA VULGARIS). SHOWING THE SIZE OF THE FOUR YOUNGEST YEAR-CLASSES IN JUNE
About natural size

3. AMERICAN EEL (ANGUILLA ROSTRATA). SHOWING THE SIZE OF THE TWO YOUNGEST YEAR-CLASSES IN JUNE
Natural size

Three of Johann Schmidt's images showing the development of the American and European eels.

thousands of dollars in cash in their pockets, paying $500 per lb (0.45 kg), did not last long. The numbers of glass eels entering Japanese rivers suddenly rose, for unknown reasons. This, combined with what could be imported from Europe, was enough to make it unnecessary to buy them in the States. No interested buyers were waiting on the river banks of New Jersey estuaries when glass eel prices fell to around $15 per lb. At the same time, concern about eel stocks and the unregulated nature of the business prompted states to ban glass eel fishing. By 2007 Maine was the only state where it was still legal to fish for glass eels. New licences are issued and old ones are renewed. People who went out at night to net them hung in through the lean years, and in 2005 the price shot up again. Maine had 510 registered glass eel fishermen and fisherwomen in 2007.

A local market for glass eels exists in some European countries – primarily Spain and England, where they are held in high esteem by diners – but most of the hundreds of tonnes of glass eels captured each year are shipped on to Chinese eel farms where they will be raised to *kabayaki* size for the Japanese market.[24] The prices that the Chinese are willing to pay are so high that most people prefer to sell them rather than eat them. In Spain, for instance, people used traditionally to eat them around the Christmas season, and what was left over they threw to the pigs. But for the past 30 years or so the market price for *angulas* (glass eels) has been climbing steadily, and now 1 lb of them can cost 70 euros at a local market. Even if only a quarter-pound are needed to make a serving, that is a pretty expensive first course to put on a table, and even more so now that imitation glass eels called *gulas*, made from a *surimi* paste of cheap fish shaped to look like a glass eel, are widely available at a fraction of the price.

Most of the eels captured when they are entering Europe's rivers will wind up in China where they will be raised to adulthood

An eel tureen and stand, made in England of soft-paste porcelain, c. 1755–8.

and an edible size, and shipped to Japan. In 2007 prices were back up to high levels, with the black market river bank price up to around £300 a kilo. Poaching of glass eels in France's rivers is widespread, and the French call the baby eels *l'or blanc*. The London *Times* reported, in December 2007, that two brothers had illegally taken glass eels out of the Loire and its surrounding tributaries for ten years, and had collected over 270 kg (600 lb) of glass eels. At more than 1,500 glass eels to a pound, that is 6 million eels that did not reach sexual maturity. Much of the glass eel traffic with Asia has been unregulated, and revenues have often gone untaxed at the fisherman's end. This may change. With the inclusion of *Anguilla anguilla* under the international CITES conservation agreement, effective from 13 March 2009, export permits for glass eels must be obtained. This means that they have to have been captured legally, and their sale will be recorded. In addition, they can only be sold for export if it is determined that such a sale will not be detrimental to the survival of the species.

6 Cultured Eel, Cultural Eel

If you dipped a hand
they'd slipper over your skin like snakes,
seaweed-cold, diaphanous, a quick-
silver stream of liquid glass catching
the sun like a twist in a marble.
From 'Eel-fare' by Sirial Troup[1]

The fact is that eel farming is possible, but eel culture is not. They can be raised but they cannot be bred. Not in 2009, at any rate. Scientists believe they are getting close. It is the Japanese who are closest to it, not surprisingly, as they have been working on culturing eels for decades. As the numbers of *Anguilla japonica* taken in the wild declined, scientists intensified their efforts to breed them in captivity.

Eel aquaculture efforts began in Tokyo in 1879 with the capture and cultivation of elvers, but it was not until 1931 that a trial using glass eels succeeded in growing out adults in commercial quantities.[2] Then Japanese scientists began to concentrate on getting eels to breed in captivity. It was slow going. The first task was to get the fish to produce viable eggs and milt from which larvae could be obtained, and this was not accomplished until 1974. It is done by injecting mature male and female eels with hormones and inducing sexual maturation. The scientists collected the milt and fertilized eggs with it, and two days later larvae hatched. The problem was that the larvae did not live longer than five days. For the first few days of life they fed on their own yolk sacs, but when those were consumed they quickly starved and died. It took scientists a while to develop a diet that larvae would eat.

Those first artificial reproduction efforts were primitive by today's standards among Japanese researchers. But one by one

A handful of glass eels.

Rice and eel, one of Japan's favourite combinations.

they discovered and modified each of the numerous factors influencing larval mortality, beginning with the make-up of the sperm and egg, and extending to diet, water temperature and numerous other variables. By 2002, almost 30 years after learning how to bring captive eels to sexual maturity, the numbers were getting better and the larvae were living as long as 25 days. No one knows what larvae eat in the wild. It is assumed to be some sort of miniscule zooplankton that they consume while on their long drifts, but scientists have had little luck feeding them zooplankton in captivity. Different feeds were developed and the larvae were kept alive beyond the time they consumed their yolk sacs, but they did not live long enough to be reared to the glass eel stage. They were still dying as larvae.

Finally, it was announced in 2004 that larvae had been kept alive for 250 days, reaching a length of 50–60 millimetres (2–2.5 inches), by using a diet of a slurry made from shark egg yolks, enhanced by supplements of krill hydrolysate, soybean peptide, vitamins and minerals. These larvae not only thrived, but the largest of them metamorphosed into glass eels, a huge step in the march towards successful eel aquaculture.[3] By 2008 Japanese biologists were said to have grown a yellow eel, but if so they had yet to publish their data, and they were still far from an acceptable larval survival rate. In addition, no sooner did they find something that seemed to stimulate the appetites of leptocephali than sharks became an endangered species, and it was clear that shark eggs would not work as a basis for a commercial larvae feed.[4] The feeding process was in any case hardly adaptable to large-scale aquaculture. The shark-egg paste had to be spread on the bottom of the pens six times a day for an hour, and then the uneaten slurry had to be flushed out after each feeding.

Another problem remaining to be resolved is that the way the larvae have grown in the Japanese experiments does not seem to exactly mirror the way they would grow in the wild. The proportion of their heads to their bodies is different from wild larvae, and they frequently appear too long and too skinny.[5] What this might portend for adult eels developed from these larvae is not known. However, many of the most serious obstacles to breeding and raising eels have been overcome, and it is not a far reach to imagine that *Anguilla japonica* may eventually be cultivated for domestic consumption.

Another major question so far unanswered is how cultured eels will taste. The Japanese have no problem with the taste of

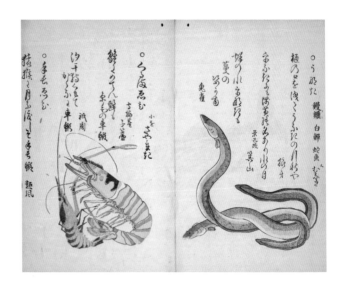

Japanese lobsters and eels from *Umi no sachi* (*The Bounty of the Sea*), 1778.

the eels raised in China from wild-captured glass eels and elvers, but studies have shown that, as with salmon, a much higher degree of fat occurs in the muscles of farm-raised eel than those taken from the wild.[6] This, even though along with catfish and salmon, is said to provide the most calories of any fish, more than a thousand per kilo.[7] When eels are finally bred and raised in captivity, it is likely that they will taste different from their wild counterparts. Will they be edible? Stay tuned.

Europeans are far behind the Japanese, but efforts to culture *Anguilla anguilla* are also underway. The Danes and the Dutch are the furthest along, again not surprisingly because they are among the top three producers of farmed eel in Europe. The Dutch grew some 3.36 million kilograms (7.4 million lb) of eels in 2000, and the Danes some 2.6 million kilograms (5.8 million lb).[8] French researchers were the first to successfully induce sexual maturation in males, in 1936, and in females in 1964. In the

1980s larvae were produced for the first time, by a Russian team, and they survived for 3.5 days. It was not until 2006 that a Danish research team led by the Technical University of Denmark succeeded in producing larvae that lived for up to twelve days.[9] The most important thing about this was that it meant the larvae were eating their egg sacs and continuing to take in nutrition after the sac was gone.

Still, the Danish team has also encountered problems at every step of the process. Once they had successfully produced larvae, they were still unable to engender predictably the mass hatchings of 50,000–100,000 viable larvae necessary for commercial farming. For all the progress made in unlocking the secrets of an eel's life, it was still the case in 2008 that the only farm-raised eels reaching the market were those that were captured in the wild, either as glass eels, or juvenile yellow eels, and grown out to eating size. Over 200,000 kilos – at more than 2,000 to a kilo – of glass eels are sold each year to farming operations.[10] Farming eels is big business in a number of places around the world and the person who comes up with a way to breed *Anguilla anguilla* and grow their larvae out to market-size eels will have a gold mine, but until then the pressure on the resource will continue to be enormous.

Until very recently Asian eel farms were hungry for seed stock and ready to buy anywhere around the world. It is generally agreed that a substantial number of these sales go unreported. Prices are frequently high and often paid in cash. The Food and Agriculture Organization (FAO) report on capture-based aquaculture concluded in 2004: 'Glass eel supply channels are very complex. In general the international market is supplied by Japanese and European glass eels, but recently also by American eels at low levels. Worldwide, both legal sales and black markets for glass eels are thriving and there are conflicts between the catch data and market prices, and a general lack of any official data on this market sector, which for eels is the most important.'[11]

In 1997, the report states, France exported over 226,000 kg (500,000 lb) of glass eels to Asia, and Danish catches were estimated at 454,000 kg (1 million lb). In 0.45 kilograms (1 lb) of glass eels there are between one and two thousand individuals, so at a minimum the annual European export would amount to hundreds of millions of glass eels, themselves survivors of an arduous three-year journey over which they lost many of their brothers and sisters. These baby eels will grow up and be eaten, removed from the reproductive pool of eels. The past two decades, and the ferocious human predation of the world's glass eels, may have mortally affected the spawning stock.

Glass eels are delicate creatures and it is estimated that 20 per cent of those captured die before even reaching an aquaculture facility.[12] They are frequently killed either by compression in a net or inadequate care taken when handling and transporting them. Those that do survive to arrive at a farm still face a series of life-threatening obstacles before growing large enough to bring to market. Eels are not easy to farm compared to many other species. While a lot of eels can be grown in a relatively small space, they are vulnerable to temperature changes, low oxygen content in the water and disease. Water quality has to be monitored and uneaten food must not be allowed to accumulate on the bottom of the pen or pool. Eels are picky eaters, and substantial numbers will not eat in captivity, or will only eat in reduced quantities, apparently finding it easier to endure malnutrition than to adapt. Those with growth rates below a certain level need to be culled so food will go only to those animals that can later be sold. Eels, like most farm-raised fish, are susceptible to stress, which weakens them and often leads to an outbreak of disease, and there are plenty of diseases waiting to afflict them. The FAO report lists more than two dozen common ones.

The numbers of eels being caught are in steep decline, as the number of eels produced by aquaculture grow-out operations continues to climb. This is, obviously, an untenable situation, and how long the market can function with decreasing supply and increasing demand remains to be seen. In 2000 the value of farm-raised European eels was put at about $80 million, with farming going on in eight EU countries. While eel farming is not easy it is potentially lucrative, and has some advantages over farming other species of fish. One is that the water can be

Straw eel ladder along the River Bann, 2001.

Production line, Lough Neagh. Fisherman's Cooperative Society Processing Plant, 2001.

recirculated, minimizing environmental impact, although wastes and uneaten food do require disposal. Another important advantage over other cultivated fish is that the eel requires little space. A profitable eel farm can be contained inside a standard warehouse. These often have low lighting and big, rectangular concrete basins filled with water and eels, which are divided according to size. Slowly, their green, brown bodies glide through the water, endlessly circling their pens in the shadows. Some of the basins hold eels 15 centimetres (6 inches) long, others big, ropy beasts as thick as a man's arm.

Europe's total production of farmed eel in 2000 was some 10.4 million kg (23 million lb). As with everything else having to deal with eels, the Asian figures are much higher, with those countries producing about 204 million kg (450 million lb) of farm-raised fish in the same year.[13] Nowhere has the disappearing stocks of wild fish around the world had more repercussions than in Japan. In the 1980s the Japanese began coming to China to encourage and invest in fish farming, and eels were high on the list. Japan needed more farmed fish than it had land to fill with water. China, on the other hand, had plenty of space. The idea fitted nicely into the nation's developing embrace of capitalism and huge fish farms developed in a number of places. By 2007 Chinese government figures reported more than 4.5 million fish farmers in the country and China has become the world's only nation where more fish are produced on farms than are taken from the wild.

In 2000 some 200 million eels were farmed there. Aquaculture in general, and farming eels in particular, is big business in China. Unfortunately, two of the vast nation's most pressing growth problems dovetail on the eel farms: water availability and pollution. Through good times and bad, economic upturns and downturns, the Japanese market for eel has been constant, with some 60 per cent of the Japanese annual consumption coming from Chinese farms. But clean water is in short supply in many of the regions with the most intense aquaculture, with industrial and agricultural contamination a frequent problem. Added to this are the effluents from the fish farms themselves, full of faecal matter, along with food, drug and pesticide residues, and the water quality is often poor, the fish are stressed, fungal and viral diseases break out among them, and more chemicals are poured into the water to treat them. In June 2007 the US Food and Drug Administration banned the importation of eels from China unless they were certified to be free of harmful residues.[14] The ban was initiated after inspectors identified traces of veterinary drugs in the eels, particularly malachite green chloride, a chemical agent used to treat parasitical and fungal diseases in fish. It is a synthetic dye used to colour a wide range of products such as silk, wool, leather, cotton and paper. It is also a suspected human carcinogen, believed to increase incidences of thyroid and breast cancers in women and testicular cancer in men, according to the journal *Food and Chemical Toxicology*.[15] Nitrofuran, an antibacterial used in Chinese eel farm waters, is another known carcinogen that turned up.

The Chinese government protested that the ban was the result of distorted media reports, and protectionist policies, but also announced that it was placing stricter controls on farmed fish and would monitor them. The market for Chinese eels took its first serious blow since it was developed. In Japan consumers demanded home-grown eels, even though they sold for twice the price of those imported from China. In other Asian countries, and in the EU, inspections of eels coming from China was stepped up. By early 2008 one online newsletter from an English marketer of glass eels reported that for the first time in eel farming history the Chinese had a backlog of eels building up, and were not buying all they could from Europe.[16]

For many fishing folk the idea that eel might be delicious is plausible, but the task of skinning one before cooking it is daunting. To the uninitiated eel is just another of those fish that is 'too much trouble'. The eel, like the catfish, is easily skinned – it needs only be nailed to a board or a tree, then a cut is made around its neck and the skin gripped with a pliers or in a strong fist and pulled downwards, sliding off the eel's body like a peel off a banana. At that point the successful sniggler will generally cook the meat and throw away the skin. Mistake – eel skin is not a trash item. A tanned eel skin makes a fine leather, and has done so for many centuries.

Smoked eels.

Eel skin is remarkable of itself, regardless of its commercial possibilities. An eel's gills are quite small, and it does a significant amount of its breathing through its skin. It has a remarkable ability to absorb moisture, and this plus the protection of the mucous that covers it keeps the skin moist enough for an eel to breathe through, and also means that an eel can spend considerable time on dry land. Eels have scales but they are so fine that they're not evident to the naked eye, and for this the Jewish rabbis grouped them with the scaleless fish not to be eaten. Eel skin is also marvellously adaptable, able to withstand the process of osmosis, the huge change in water pressure that takes place between fresh and salt water.

The leather made of eel skin is light and durable and is known as 'the silk of the oceans, one of the lightest yet strongest of leathers', according to the website toadtraders.com, which sells eel-skin products. 'Variations in colour and other markings such as scars, bites and fat wrinkles capture the natural beauty of the eel and make each product unique.' It has a natural sheen to it and is smooth and pleasant to the touch. These qualities have been appreciated for many centuries. The anthropologist Frank Speck witnessed Maine's Penobscot Indians making use of it: 'Besides lines of braided rawhide and of basswood fibre, ropes of braided eel-skin are known. To make them, large eel skins in the raw state are selected and cut in strips about an inch wide then braided in three ply.'[17]

These days eel skin is still used, although infrequently enough to make it almost a curiosity in the leather trade. A few odd items are still made with it, and online a number of companies offer eel-skin Bible cases, and Zondervan Publishing offers a Bible bound in it. Most of the eel-skin products offered for sale today, however, are purses, bags and wallets, with a smattering of handmade high-end items like $500 boots. George W. Bush had a penchant for cowboy boots made of eel skin. For himself he had them made embossed with the presidential seal, and to his friends he gave pairs that carried his initials.[18]

Eel-skin leather has long been appreciated by Yankees. In early nineteenth-century New York, wearing an eel skin around one's queue – a braid of hair worn long behind – was favoured among free African-American swells and sharp dressers. They disdained the modest discretion of the older generation of free African-Americans. 'Whereas the respectables met in the quiet decorum of their sitting rooms, the newcomers joined together in smoke-filled gaming houses and noisy midnight frolics,' wrote Ira Berlin in *Many Thousands Gone*. 'Their boisterous lifestyle, colourful dress, plaited hair, eel-skin queues, and swaggering gait scandalized the respectables.'[19]

However, race did not always have a role in tying a queue with an eel skin, and the practice is cited in W. Jeffrey Bolster's *Black Jacks: African-American Seamen in the Age of Sail* as an example of a habit belonging to an occupational subculture of both black and white seamen in New York. 'In the middle of the eighteenth century, many black men from Long Island wore queues secured with an eel skin, a style favoured by white naval sailors well into the nineteenth century . . . Whether African Americans or whites first wore their hair this way is moot; what is significant is the cultural predisposition that led both groups to adopt a unique style.'[20]

For millennia eel skin was best known for one of its ambivalent qualities: it made good whips. The whips made of it were used on humans as well as animals. The Romans left records of an eel-skin whip being used to flog children and adults, according to William Radcliffe in *Fishing from the Earliest Times*. The French satirist François Rabelais wrote in the sixteenth century: 'Whereupon his master gave him such a sound thrashing with

Mick Jenrick with eels, at his stand in Billingsgate market.

an eel-skin, that his own would have been worth naught for bag-pipes.'[21] An eel-skin whip was a common possession in Anglo-Saxon households, and these forefathers were well acquainted with the uses of the lash. On 24 April 1663 Samuel Pepys wrote in his diary of daily life in London: 'With my salt eele, went down in the parler, and there got my boy and did beat him.'[22]

Eel skin is also used for more esoteric purposes. In the same way that the striped bass season in New England supports a small capture fishery for the bait market, so a small commercial outlet for eel skin exists to serve the same public. The practice of shaping a wooden or metal plug, covering it with an eel skin and attaching a treble hook beneath its head and another beneath its mid-section is an old one when fishing for striped bass or bluefish along the New England coast. Eel skin lures are used both in casting and trolling, and have a small but faithful market. 'Every once in a while you'll find an old-timer casting an eel-skin plug', wrote Nelson Bryant in a 1988 *New York Times* piece. 'The plug so rigged is usually a surface swimmer such as the Danny or Atom. One removes the hooks so the skin can be slipped over the plug. A couple of inches of the skin is left hanging beyond the tail of the plug, and the front end, trimmed to the proper length, is lashed behind the plug's metal lip.'[23]

Not all the uses of eel skin were of a punishing or painful variety. Its healing properties were also celebrated. Giovanni Bonaveri wrote, in 1761, of its curative powers, according to Tom Fort in *The Book of Eels*. Bonaveri, who travelled to Comacchio in the mid-eighteenth century, believed that the skin, dried and ground to a powder, could aid in the passing of stones, and when applied by funnel to the vagina it would prevent the slackening of the muscles therein. Fort also records that eel skin was used in ancient times to make door hinges and membranes for filtering liquids. Not so long ago, he wrote, it was still used in the Fens of eastern England to ward off illness, by both men and women, who wore strips of eel skin as garters: 'Strips of skin were dried in the sun, greased with fat, placed in a linen bag stuffed with thyme, lavender, and marsh mint, then

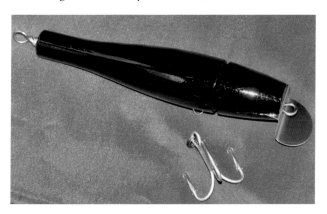

Eel-skin fishing lure.

buried under the peat for the summer, before being dug up, greased again, polished with a smooth stone and declared ready to be tied around Fenland legs.'[24]

Gwenn-Aël Bolloré reports that in France eel fat was also valued for its curative properties, among them the ability to cure an ear ache and to reduce haemorrhoids, as well as to apply on parts affected by gout. She also adds that it is recommended for a slackening of the vaginal muscles and that eel liver in a glass of wine was recommended by an English writer in the late eighteenth century as helpful to women as they went into labour.[25] However, one physical effect that eels can have on humans is dangerous: their blood is toxic and can cause some serious reactions. Places where eel are chopped up in number have an emergency eyewash in place, so that should a bit of blood splash into an eye it can be flooded out. Otherwise it can temporarily blind a person or permanently damage an eyeball. Rabbits injected with serum made from eel blood die. Its poison works in two ways, according to Léon Bertin: through cytolytic action, which destroys cells, and neurotoxic action, affecting the nervous system. Bertin described it: 'With a strong dose, 0.1 to 0.2 cc. per kg. of rabbit, the subject shows violent convulsions and within a few minutes breathing ceases and this is followed by heart failure.'[26]

Eels are such ordinary and out-of-sight creatures that they rarely draw attention, but they do appear occasionally in various cultural manifestations from around the globe. Twentieth-century novels have occasionally turned a spotlight on them. *The Tin Drum* by Günter Grass has a memorable scene set on a beach. Little Oskar the narrator is there with his parents and his mother's lover, and they watch as a man pulls a freshly severed horse's head to shore. The fisherman picks a couple of dozen small eels off the head, then squeezes it and a half dozen bigger ones ooze out as he squeezes:

Father William balances an eel on his nose, an illustration by John Tenniel for *Alice's Adventures in Wonderland* (1865).

With the help of his rubber boot he wrenched the horse's mouth open and forced a club between the jaws, so that the great yellow horse teeth seemed to be laughing. And when the longshoreman . . . reached both hands into the horse's gullet and pulled out two at once, both of them as thick and long as a man's arm, my mother's jaws were also torn asunder: she disgorged her whole breakfast, pouring out lumpy egg white and threads of egg yolk mingled in lumps of bread soaked in *café au lait* over the stones of the breakwater.[27]

Graham Swift's *Waterland*, set in the watery marshes of the Fens, is a virtual textbook on eel biology and migration and capture, woven into a novel of place and people. Its protagonist is a history teacher, teaching his last-ever class of students about their own history, inextricably bound up to the eel's, in the waterland of the Fens that they share with *Anguilla anguilla*. In a

S. ITISBERGA Virgo, Pipini III. Galliæ Regis filia, et Caroli Magni Imp. soror, condita est in monte eius nomine celebri, apud Aeriam Artesiæ opidum, ibíque frequenti peregrinantium concursu honoratur.

chapter called 'About the Eel' he tells the wonderful story of the discovery of how they reproduce, and celebrates Johannes Schmidt's relentless search for eel larvae. 'Who has heard of Johannes Schmidt?' the teacher asks his students. 'It is said that modern times do not have their Sinbads, and Jasons, let alone their Drakes and Magellans, that the days of the great sea-quests went out with Cook. Johannes Schmidt is an exception.'[28]

In the visual arts, eels have also occasionally drawn an artist's eye. The painter William Sidney Mount, from Setauket, New York, painted *Eel Spearing at Setauket*, a young white boy and a middle-aged black woman in a small punt on a bucolic pond, she with the spear raised to strike, he looking on, both appearing to imagine the eel hidden beneath the surface as lunch. Lunch might also be much on the minds of the family in

154

Jean-Baptiste-Camille Corot's *The Eel Gatherers*, painted in 1865. It shows them passing the day beside a deeply shaded rural stream, a mother and two daughters idling beside the water, a young boy high up a tree beside them, and a bit downstream a man in a white shirt with sleeves rolled up stands in the shallows, bent over looking for eels. Edouard Manet also appreciated the lovely curves and sheen of the eel, amply demonstrated in his remarkable *Still-life with Eel and Red Mullet*.

Something about eels seems to inspire the bizarre among photographers. Perhaps no single photo of those taken by the controversial Brooklyn photographer of nightmares, Joel-Peter Witkin, has engendered so much reaction as his *Woman Breastfeeding an Eel*, which shows a large-breasted, masked woman doing just that. Then there is a series of eel photographs by Francesca Woodman, another New York resident, who used her striking black-and-white work as a way to make form of her

William Sidney Mount, *Eel Spearing at Setauket*, 1845, oil on canvas.

Still-life with Eel and Red Mullet, by Edouard Manet, 1864, oil on canvas.

inner torment, and who killed herself at age 23. In her eel photographs a nude woman lying on a mosaic-tiled floor curves her body around a bowl holding eels curved around themselves in the bowl.

Eel have shown up in moving pictures as well. German director Volker Schlöndorff, in his award-winning film adaptation of *The Tin Drum*, did justice to the scene of fishing for eels with a horse's head. Not surprisingly, it was a Japanese director who made a movie that was actually titled *The Eel*. Shohei Imamura's 1997 film is a dark story of love and revenge, set in a small eel-fishing village.

While eels may not appear all that frequently in popular culture, fishing for them does constitute the economic lifeblood of towns and villages around the world. These eel-based communities stretch right round the globe from the wetlands of the North Carolina coast's Neuse River, to Northern Ireland's eel fishermen's cooperative, to the glass eel fishery in England's River Severn and the Orió River in Spain's Basque country, to France's Loire River, or the waterlands of Comacchio in Italy, to numerous rivers in China and Japan. All told it is a multi-billion dollar business and while its centres of activity may not be huge metropolises they are tied together by the sinuous bonds of the eel. By and large, these capitals of the eel world are far off the beaten track. They, like the eel itself, could disappear and 99.9 per cent of the world's citizens would never remark their absence. But the world would be a poorer place if it did not have room for people who like to work alone and make their livings from whatever body of water they live near. Ours would be a

A drawer of eels at Mick Jenrick's stand at Billingsgate market.

'Tied Up in Knots' by Victòria Rabal i Merola.

smaller, meaner, more constricted world if it could not accommodate those people who fish for eel, who mind their own business and expect us to do the same.

Just as it would be a meaner world if it no longer offered the simple conditions needed to support eel life. They do not demand much. This ever-so-ordinary, rarely noticed animal only wants a chance to spend its days and nights eating, growing and resting at the muddy bottom of some body of water, far from human eyes, just as it has done for years, centuries and millennia. In reality it is much less ever-so-ordinary than our own selves. An eel changes not only its form but also its body at a cellular level three times during its lifetime, going from a salt-water to a freshwater fish and back. They make our life cycle seem monotonous: all we do is pass infancy to old age in the same growing then deteriorating form. Imagine if we spent part

A Moray eel depicted in water-colours by an unknown painter at Port Jackson, New South Wales, Australia, *c.* 1788–97. The inscription notes that the Aboriginal people call it a 'Kaan'.

of our lives able to drink from the sea, or part of our allotted spans as neither men nor women. An eel's life encompasses all that and more – 2,000-mile swims, as well as periods of virtual hibernation for months at a time.

Eels are fascinating and wonderful creatures. We need to treat them with due respect and gratitude for their role in providing an ancient source of protein for our own species. We owe them what protection we can provide against those threats to their existence from our fellow humans. The fate of the eel is likely to be our own. If eels are allowed to thrive, so much the better. If the world reaches a state in which there is no place in it for *Anguilla*, for that common and wonderful fish, then it is likely there will not be much of a place in it for humans either.

Here's to the eel.

Timeline of the Eel

100 MYA	6000 BC	800 BC	450 BC
Lebanon's eel fossils date from the middle Cretaceous period, when dinosaurs roamed the earth	Remains of fish spears and eel traps at Mount Sandel, Northern Ireland, illustrate the presence of eels in the human diet	The Greek oral epic the *Iliad*, in which Homer sings of eels nibbling the flesh of the recently dead	Herodotus reports that Egyptians worship the eel as a minor deity

AD 170	1086	*c.* 1250	*c.* 1260
The Roman poet Oppianus holds that the slime coating eels is worked into a froth when two of them rub together, and from this come baby eels	The Domesday Book records that Evesham Abbey's eel fishery yields as many as 2,000 eels at a time	Hot pasties are sold on Paris streets stuffed with a variety of minced meats, including pork, pigeon, goose, and eel	Albertus Magnus asserts in his *Book of Animals* that eels are viviparous, giving birth to live young

1852	1874	1877	1901	1904
In London's Billingsgate Market alone, over 1.1 million lb (500,000 kg) of eel are sold	Polish naturalist Szymon Syrski publishes his discovery of the male eel's genitalia in the *Proceedings* of the Vienna Imperial Academy of Sciences	Sigmund Freud fails to duplicate Syrski's work and definitively identify the male reproductive organs, although he guesses correctly their position	Two North American scientists, Carl Eigenmann and Clarence Kennedy describe two larvae of American eel caught off the New England coast	Danish oceanographer Johannes Schmidt begins his search for the eel's breeding ground and eel larvae

411 BC	350 BC	300 BC

Aristophanes has Lysistrata call for the destruction of all of Boetia except for its eels, reputed to have been the best in ancient Greece

Aristotle gives the first explanation of eel reproduction, erroneously declaring that eels generate spontaneously from mud

Philetaerus expresses the ancient world's regard for eels when he writes that he fears death because the dead cannot eat eels

1500	1621	1692	1777

The sale of an entire year's eels from Comacchio, some 45,000 gold escudos, pays for the construction of the Este family's fabulous Palazzo dei Diamanti in Ferrara

The Native American named Tisquantum shows vast compassion and forgiveness and teaches the *Mayflower* Pilgrims how to catch eels

Antonie van Leeuwenhoek publishes his complete support of viviparity, mistaking parasites for young about to be born

Italian biologist Carlos Mondini locates the frilled reproductive organs of the female eel

1924	1974	1978	2004	2007

Schmidt report *The Breeding Places of the Eel* reveals the larval phases of an eel's life

First breeding of eels in laboratory takes place in Japan

The current British record-holder's prize catch is an 11 lb 2 oz (5.05 kg) eel taken at Kingfisher Lake, Hampshire

Eel larvae kept alive for 250 days in captivity, some of which metamorphose into glass eels

European eel added to CITES list of species needing special protection

References

INTRODUCTION

1 Aristotle, *Historia Animalum*, trans. D'Arcy Wentworth Thompson (Oxford, 1910).
2 Johannes Schmidt, 'The Breeding Places of the Eel', *Annual Report of the Smithsonian Institute* (1924), p. 283.
3 William Dekker, 'Eel Stocks Dangerously Close To Collapse', www.ices.dk/marineworld/eel.asp.
4 Francesca Ottolenghi et al., *Capture-Based Aquaculture* (Rome, 2004), pp. 30–36.
5 Alexandre Dumas, *Le Grand Dictionnaire de Cuisine*, trans. Alan and Jane Davidson (London, 1978), p. 118.
6 John Goodwin, *The Pilgrim Republic* (Boston, 1888), p. 127.
7 Richard Schweid, *Consider the Eel* (Cambridge, 2004), pp. 92–5.
8 'Eel Farming in the Netherlands', *Aquaculture Magazine* (July/August 1998), p. 52.
9 William Dekker, 'Eel Stocks Dangerously Close To Collapse', www.ices.dk/marineworld/eel.asp.
10 Masaya Katoh and Masahiro Kobayashi, 'Aquaculture and Genetic Structure in the Japanese Eel', *Anguilla Japonica. UJNR Technical Report No. 30* (2000), p. 87.
11 Léon Bertin, *Eels: A Biological Study* (New York, 1957), pp. 170–71.
12 Hiromi Ohta, 'Artificial Fertilization Using Testicular Spermatozoa in the Japanese Eel Anguilla Japonica', *Fisheries Science*, LXIII/3 (1997), pp. 393–6.
13 Ottolenghi et al., *Capture-Based Aquaculture*, p. 31.

1 THE EEL QUESTION

1 Oppianus, *Halieuticks of the Nature of Fishes*, trans. John Jones, Book I (Oxford, 1722), p. 5.
2 Leopold Jacoby, 'The Eel Question', in *United States Commission of Fish and Fisheries, Report of the Commissioner for 1879* (Washington, DC, 1882), p. 463.
3 Tom Fort, *The Book of Eels* (London, 2002), p. 120.
4 Joshua Slocum, *Sailing Alone Around the World* (London, 1963), p. 246.
5 J. Larry Wilson and David Turner, 'Occurrence of the American Eel in the Holston River, Tennessee', *Journal of the Tennessee Academy of Science*, LVII/1 (January 1982), pp. 63–4.
6 Aristotle, *Historia Animalum*, trans. D'Arcy Wentworth Thompson (Oxford, 1910), Book VI, chapter 16.
7 Fort, *Book of Eels*, pp. 63–4.
8 George Brown Goode, *The Fisheries and Fishery Industries of the United States* (Washington, DC, 1884), p. 638.
9 Izaak Walton and Charles Cotton, *The Compleat Angler* (London, 1960).
10 David Cairncross, *The Origin of the Silver Eel* (London, 1862), p. 2.
11 Jacoby, 'The Eel Question', p. 465.
12 Goode, *The Fisheries and Fishery Industries of the United States*, p. 640.
13 Quoted in Peter Newton, *Freud: From Youthful Dream To Mid-Life Crisis* (New York, 1995), p. 76.
14 Francine Jacobs, *The Freshwater Eel* (New York, 1973), pp. 12–14.
15 Quoted in Fort, *Book of Eels*, p. 70.
16 Johannes Schmidt, 'The Breeding Places of the Eel', *Annual Report of the Smithsonian Institute* (1924), p. 281.
17 Ibid., p. 305.
18 Elizabeth Pennisi, 'Much Ado about Eels', *BioScience* (1989), p. 596.
19 Schmidt, 'Breeding Places of the Eel', p. 313.
20 F. W. Tesch, 'The Sargasso Sea Expedition, 1979', *Helgoländer Meeresuntersuchungen*, XXXV (1982), pp. 263–77.
21 Elizabeth Pennisi, 'Gone Eeling', *Science News* (1991), pp. 297–8.

22 James McCleave, interview with the author, July 2000.

23 'Investigating the Mysteries of the Eel', *Insight* (International Council for the Exploration of the Sea), XLIV/5 (September 2007).

2 ENDANGERED EEL

1 Quoted in C. David Badham, *Prose Halieutics or Ancient and Modern Fish Tattle* (London, 1854), p. 390.

2 Peter Lamothe et al., 'Homing and Movement of Yellow-Phase American Eels in Freshwater Ponds', *Environmental Biology of Fishes*, LVIII (2000), pp. 393–9.

3 Friedrich-Wilhelm Tesch, *The Eel* (London, 1977), pp. 53–6.

4 Ibid., pp. 154–7.

5 S. J. Parker, 'Homing Ability and Home Range of Yellow-Phase American Eels in a Tidally Dominated Estuary', *Journal of Marine Biological Association UK* (1995), pp. 127–40.

6 Tesch, *The Eel*, pp. 219–20.

7 Ibid., p. 171.

8 Ibid., p. 211.

9 Ibid., pp. 172–7.

10 Brian Crawford, *Catch More Eels* (London, 1975), p. 35.

11 Gene S. Helfman, 'Spinning for their Supper', *Natural History* (May 1995), pp. 26–9.

12 Richard Schweid, *Consider the Eel* (Cambridge, 2004), p. 104.

13 Uwe Kils, interview with the author, May 2001.

14 William Dekker, 'Eel Stocks Dangerously Close To Collapse', www.ices.dk/marineworld/eel.asp.

15 Martin Castonguay et al., 'Why is Recruitment of the American Eel, *Anguilla rostrata*, Declining in the St Lawrence River and Gulf?', *Canadian Journal of Fisheries and Aquatic Sciences*, LI/2 (February 1994), pp. 479–88.

16 'Anguilla', in Government of Canada, Species at Risk Public Registry, available at www.sararegistry.gc.ca/search/advSearch Results_e.cfm?stype=species&advkeywords=Anguilla, accessed 4 June 2008.

17 'American Eels', Gulf of Maine Council on the Marine
    Environment, available at
    www.gulfofmaine.org/council/publication/American_eel_low-
    res.pdf. accessed 4 June 2008.

18 Heather Bell and Diana Weaver, *The Northeast Fish Rapper –
    Newsletter of the Northeastern Division of the American Fisheries
    Society* (March 2007), p. 9.

19 Tom Fort, *The Book of Eels* (London, 2002), p. 268.

20 William McElroy, personal communication to author, February
    2001.

21 C. M. Couillard et al., 'Correlations between Pathological Changes
    and Chemical Contamination in American Eels, Anguilla
    Rostrata, from the St Lawrence River', *Canadian Journal of
    Fisheries and Aquatic Sciences* (1997), pp. 1916–27.

22 Jacob de Boer et al., '8-Year Study on the Elimination of PCBs and
    Other Organochlorine Compounds from Eel (*Anguilla anguilla*)
    under Natural Conditions', *Environmental Science and Technology*
    (1994), pp. 2242–8.

23 Tesch, *The Eel*, p. 78.

24 Atlantic States Marine Fisheries Commission, 'Fishery
    Management Plan for American Eel, Fishery Management
    Report' (October 1999), p. 51.

25 A. T. Haro et al., 'Simulated Effects of Hydroelectric Project
    Regulation on Mortality of American Eels', *American Fisheries
    Society Symposium* (2003), pp. 357–65.

26 'American Eels', Gulf of Maine Council on the Marine Environment.

27 B. Knights, 'A Review of the Possible Impacts of Long-term
    Oceanic and Climate Changes and Fishing Mortality on
    Recruitment of Anguillid Eels of the Northern Hemisphere',
    Science of the Total Environment (2003), pp. 237–44.

28 'American Eels', Gulf of Maine Council on the Marine
    Environment.

29 Atlantic States Marine Fisheries Commission, *Stock Assessment
    Report No. 06-01* (2006), p. 10.

30 Joint EIFAC/ICES Working Group on Eels, *Report of the 2006 Session*

(2006), p. iii.

31 Dekker, 'Eel Stocks Dangerously Close to Collapse' (see reference 14 above for source.

32 Personal communication with Oliver Kennedy, director of the Lough Neagh Fishermen's Cooperative, October 2007.

33 Fort, *Book of Eels*, pp. 182–95.

34 Folco Cecchini, ed., *Sorella Anguila* (Bologna, 1990), pp. 59–61.

35 Schweid, *Consider the Eel*, pp. 146–7.

36 Francesca Ottolenghi et al., *Capture-Based Aquaculture* (Rome, 2004), p.35.

37 Dekker, 'Eel Stocks Dangerously Close to Collapse'.

38 Council of the European Union, Council Regulation 1100/2007 of 18 September 2007 establishing measures for the recovery of the stock of European eel.

39 M. C. Sullivan et al., '*Anguilla rostrata* Glass Eel Ingress into Two US East Coast Estuaries: Patterns, Processes and Implications for Adult Eel Abundance', *Journal of Fish Biology* (2006), pp. 1081–101.

3 CLASSICAL EEL

1 In Seamus Heaney, *A Door into the Dark* (London, 1985), p. 45.

2 In William Radcliffe, *Fishing from the Earliest Times* (Chicago, 1974), p. 249.

3 Gwenn-Aël Bolloré, *La Saga de l'Anguille* (Paris, 1986), p. 17.

4 Tom Fort, *The Book of Eels* (London, 2002), p. 35.

5 J. C. Wilcocks, *The Sea-Fisherman* (Guernsey, 1875), p. 73.

6 Homer, *The Iliad*, trans. Robert Fitzgerald (Garden City, NY, 1974), p. 499.

7 In Alexandre Dumas, *Dumas on Food*, ed. Alan and Jane Davidson (London, 1978), p. 118.

8 Bolloré, *La Saga de l'Anguille*, p. 9.

9 In Radcliffe, *Fishing from the Earliest Times*, pp. 247–8.

10 C. David Badham, *Prose Halieutics or Ancient and Modern Fish Tattle* (London, 1854), p. 382.

11 Ibid. p. 371.

12 Radcliffe, *Fishing from the Earliest Times*, p. 250.

13 Waverly Root, *Food* (New York, 1980), p. 116.

14 In Badham *Prose Halieutics*, p. 380 (fn).

15 Ibid., p. 380.

16 In Radcliffe, *Fishing from the Earliest Times*, p. 248.

17 M. Gabius Apicius, *Cookery and Dining in Imperial Rome* (Chicago, 1936), p. 230.

18 Oppianus, *Halieuticks of the Nature of Fishes*; trans. John Jones, Book I (Oxford, 1722), p. 37.

19 Fort, *Book of Eels*, p. 36.

20 Arturo Bellini, 'Sullo Stato Attuale Della Produzione Anguillifera Delle Coste Tedesche del Mar Baltico e Delle Acque Continentali Nord-Germaniche', Unpublished MS, Comacchio municipal library (1903), p. 27.

21 D. G. Butler, 'Osmoregulation in North American Eels (Anguilla Rostrata LeSueur) on Land and in Freshwater: Effects of the Corpuscles of Stannius', *Journal of Comparative Physiology*, B series, CLXIX (1999), pp. 139–47.

22 In Fort, *Book of Eels*, p. 133.

23 Robert Plot, *The Natural History of Staffordshire* (Oxford, 1686), pp. 242–3.

24 Edward Jesse, *Gleanings in Natural History* (London, 1834), p. 48.

25 Francis Day, *The Fishes of Great Britain and Ireland*, vol. II (London, 1880–84), p. 243.

26 *The Goodman of Paris: A Treatise on Moral and Domestic Economy*, ed. G. G. Coulton and Eileen Power (London, 1928).

27 Dante Alighieri, *The Divine Comedy* (New York, 1996), p. 252.

28 Fort, *Book of Eels* (London, 2002), pp. 187–8.

29 Bolloré, *La Saga de l'Anguille*, p. 19.

30 In F. L. Attenborough, ed. T*he Laws of the Earliest English Kings* (Cambridge, 1922), p. 59.

31 Richard Warner, *Antiquitates Culinariae* (London, 1791).

32 W. M., *The Queen's Closet Opened: Incomparable Secrets in Physick, Chyrurgery, Preserving, and Candying, &c. Which Were Presented Unto the Queen* (London, 1655), pp. 339–40.

4 PURITANS AND VICTORIANS

1 L. A. Morrison, *A History of Windham, New Hampshire* (Boston, MA, 1883), p. 114.
2 Tom Fort, *The Book of Eels* (London, 2002), p. 46.
3 Pierre Boucher, *True and Genuine Description of New France, Commonly Called Canada* (Paris, 1664), p. 36.
4 Gabriel Sagard-Theodat, *The Long Journey To the Country of the Hurons* (Toronto, 1939), p. 270.
5 Daniel Gookin, *An Historical Account of the Indians* (Whitefish, MT, 2003), p. 150
6 Quoted in Evan Jones, *American Food: The Gastronomic Story* (Woodstock, NY, 1990), p. 5.
7 Frank Speck, *Penobscot Man* (Philadelphia, 1940), p. 96.
8 William Wood, *New England's Prospect* (1634) (Amherst, MA, 1993), p. 56.
9 John Josselyn, *Two Voyages To New England* (Cambridge, 1833), p. 275.
10 In Sandy Oliver, *Saltwater Foodways* (Mystic, CT, 1995), p. 376.
11 Hannah Glasse, *The Art of Cookery Made Plain and Easy* (London, 1747), p. 92.
12 Henry David Thoreau, *A Week on the Concord and Merrimack Rivers* (New York, 1985), p.28.
13 Mary Randolph, *The Virginia Housewife* (Washington, DC, 1824), p. 68.
14 Fort, *Book of Eels* (London, 2002), p. 175.
15 Henry Mayhew, *London Labour and the London Poor*, vol. I (London, 1861), p. 66.
16 Charles Dickens, *The Life and Adventures* of *Nicholas Nickleby* (Ware, Herts, 1995), p. 604.
17 Chris Clunn, *Eels, Pie and Mash* (London, 1995), p. 12.
18 Jim Smith, *Pie 'N' Mash: A Guide To London's Traditional Eating House* (London, 1995), p. 10.
19 Jane Grigson, *Jane Grigson's Fish Book* (London, 1993), p. 123.

1 Walt Whitman, *Leaves of Grass* (New York, 1964), p. 159.
2 'Eel: Anguilla Anguilla', Fish 'n' Tips, available at http://www.maggotdrowning.com/fish/eel.htm, accessed 5 June 2008.
3 Christopher Moriarty, *Eels: A Natural and Unnatural History* (New York, 1978), p. 29.
4 Léon Bertin, *Eels: A Biological Study* (New York, 1957), p. 46.
5 Oppianus, *Halieuticks of the Nature of Fishes*; trans. John Jones, Book XIV (Oxford, 1722), p. 171.
6 Quoted in Tom Fort, *The Book of Eels* (London, 2002), pp. 35–6.
7 Ibid., p. 34.
8 J. C. Bellamy, *Housekeeper's Guide to the Fish Market* (London, 1843).
9 G. C. Davies, *Norfolk Broad*, VI. 43 (1863), p. 157.
10 Quoted in Fort, *Book of Eels*, p. 49.
11 Clyde McKenzie Jr, *The Fisheries of Raritan Bay* (New Brunswick, NJ, 1992), pp. 20–21.
12 Frank Speck, *Penobscot Man* (Philadelphia, 1940), p. 85.
13 Wynken de Worde, *Book of Saint Albans* (1496), trans. William Van Wyck (New York, 1933), p. 46.
14 Izaak Walton and Charles Cotton, *The Compleat Angler* (London, 1960), p. 173.
15 Brian Crawford, *Fishing for Big Eels* (Big E Publications, Shropshire, 1983), p. 12.
16 Anonymous, *Athletic Sports for Boys: A Repository of Graceful Recreations for Youth* (New York, 1866), p. 145.
17 McKenzie, *The Fisheries of Raritan Bay*, p. 134.
18 Cyrus A. Adler, 'Eel Stories', *Underwater Naturalist*, XXIV/3 (2001), p. 31.
19 E. W. Gudger, 'Fishes in Water Pipes', *The American Midland Naturalist*, XLIII/2 (1950), pp. 399–403.
20 Francesca Ottolenghi et al., *Capture-Based Aquaculture* (Rome, 2004), p. 32.

21 Elaine Lies, 'Eek! Japan's Eel Fans Reel Amid Chinese Food Fears',
   Reuters (25 July 2007),
   www.reuters.com/article/latestCrisis/idUST224067.
22 Atlantic States Marine Fisheries Commission, 'Overview of Stock
   Status: American Eel, Anguilla Rostrata', available at
   www.asmfc.org.
23 Dick Hopkins, interview with the author, 2001.
24 Francesca Ottolenghi et al., *Capture-Based Aquaculture* (Rome, 2004),
   p. 33.

6 CULTURED EEL, CULTURAL EEL

1 Siriol Troup, *The River Thames in Verse: An Illustrated Anthology of
   New Poems*, ed. Val Moran (Windsor, Berkshire, 2004), p. 47.
2 Stéphane Ringuet et al., 'Eels: Their Harvest and Trade in Europe
   and Asia', *TRAFFIC Bulletin*, XIX/2 (2002), p. 11.
3 H. Tanaka et al., 'The First Production of Glass Eel in Captivity:
   Fish Reproductive Physiology Facilitates Great Progress in
   Aquaculture', *Fish Physiology and Biochemistry*, XXVIII/1–4 (2003),
   pp. 493–7.
4 Joanna Tomkiewicz, interview with the author, 2008.
5 Ibid.
6 Francesca Ottolenghi et al., *Capture-Based Aquaculture* (Rome,
   2004), p. 51.
7 Erhard Rostland, *Freshwater Fishing in Native North America*
   (Berkeley, CA, 1952), p. 4.
8 Ottolenghi, *Capture-Based Aquaculture*, p. 46.
9 Birthe Kyhn, 'A Breakthrough in Eel Research' (2007), National
   Institute of Aquatic Resources, Technical University of Denmark,
   Copenhagen, available at
   www.dfu.dtu.dk/English/News.aspx?guid=%7B634F22E2-E019-
   4378-AE3D-7B97C043EC68%7D, accessed 6 June 2008.
10 Ottolenghi, *Capture-Based Aquaculture*, p. 33.
11 Ibid., p. 37.
12 Ibid., p. 41.

13 Ibid., p. 43.

14 Julie Schmit et al., 'Chinese Fish Crisis Shows Seafood Safety Challenges', *USA Today* (Money) (28 June 2007), p. 1.

15 Sandra Culp et al., 'Carcinogenity of Malachite Green and Leucomalachite Green in B6C3F(Subset1) Mice and F344 Rats', *Journal of Food and Chemical Toxicology*, XLIV/8 (August 2006), pp. 1204–12.

16 'UK glass eels', available at www.glasseel.com/index (February 2008), accessed 7 June 2008.

17 Frank Speck, *Penobscot Man* (Philadelphia, 1940), p. 137.

18 Jim Yardley, 'Vicarious Consumption: Boots Made for Walking on Pennsylvania Avenue', *New York Times* (Business) (13 May 2001), p. 1.

19 Ira Berlin, *Many Thousands Gone: The First Two Centuries of Slavery in North America* (Cambridge, MA, 1998), p. 254.

20 W. Jeffrey Bolster, *Black Jacks: African American Seamen in the Age of Sail* (Cambridge, MA, 1998), p. 92.

21 William Radcliffe, *Fishing from the Earliest Times* (Chicago, IL, 1974), p. 262.

22 Samuel Pepys, *Diary* (London, 1983), IV, p. 109.

23 Nelson Bryant, 'Outdoors: Natural Baits', *The New York Times* (Sports) (12 September 1988).

24 Tom Fort, *The Book of Eels* (London, 2002), p. 43.

25 Gwenn-Aël Bolloré, *La Saga de l'Anguille* (Paris, 1986), p. 296.

26 Léon Bertin, *Eels: A Biological Study* (New York, 1957), p. 64.

27 Gunter Grass, *The Tin Drum*; trans. Ralph Manheim (New York, 1962), p. 150.

28 Graham Swift, *Waterland* (New York, 1983), p. 199.

Select Bibliography

Apicius, M. Gabius, *Cookery and Dining in Imperial Rome* (Chicago, 1936)

Aristotle, *Historia Animalum*, trans. D'Arcy Wentworth Thompson (Oxford, 1910

Atlantic States Marine Fisheries Commission, 'Fishery Management Plan for American Eel', *Fishery Management Report* (Washington, DC, 1999)

Badham, C. David, *Prose Halieutics or Ancient and Modern Fish Tattle* (London, 1854)

Bellini, Arturo, 'Sullo Stato Attuale Della Produzione Anguillifera Delle Coste Tedesche del Mar Baltico e Delle Acque Continentali Nord-Germaniche', unpublished MS, Municipal library, Comacchio, Italy (1903)

Bertin, Léon, *Eels: A Biological Study* (New York, 1957)

Bolloré, Gwenn-Aël, *La Saga de l'Anguille* (Paris, 1986)

Boucher, Pierre, *True and Genuine Description of New France, Commonly Called Canada* (Paris, 1664)

Butler, D. G., 'Osmoregulation in North American Eels (Anguilla Rostrata LeSueur) on Land and in Freshwater: Effects of the Corpuscles of Stannius', *Journal of Comparative Physiology B*, CLXIX (1999), pp. 139–47

Castonguay, Martin et al., 'Why is Recruitment of the American Eel, *Anguilla rostrata*, Declining in the St Lawrence River and Gulf?' *Canadian Journal of Fisheries and Aquatic Sciences*, LI/2 (February 1994), pp. 479–88

Cecchini, Folco, ed., *Sorella Anguila* (Bologna, 1990)

Clunn, Chris, *Eels, Pie and Mash* (London, 1995)

Couillard, C. M. et al., 'Correlations between Pathological Changes and Chemical Contamination in American Eels, Anguilla Rostrata, from the St Lawrence River', *Canadian Journal of Fisheries and Aquatic Sciences* (1997), pp. 1916–27

Coulton, G. G. and Eileen Power, eds, *The Goodman of Paris: A Treatise on Moral and Domestic Economy* (London, 1928)

Council of the European Union, Council Regulation 1100/2007 of 18 September 2007 establishing measures for the recovery of the stock of European Eel

Crawford, Brian, *Catch More Eels* (London, 1975)

de Boer, Jacob et al., '8-Year Study on the Elimination of PCBs and Other Organochlorine Compounds from Eel (*Anguilla anguilla*) under Natural Conditions', *Environmental Science and Technology* (1994), pp. 2242–8

Dekker, William, 'Eel Stocks Dangerously Close to Collapse' (www.ices.dk/marineworld/eel.asp)

Dumas, Alexandre, *Le Grand Dictionnaire de Cuisine*, trans. Alan and Jane Davidson (London, 1978)

Fort, Tom, *The Book of Eels* (London, 2002)

Glasse, Hannah, *The Art of Cookery Made Plain and Easy* (London, 1747)

Goode, George Brown, *The Fisheries and Fishery Industries of the United States* (Washington, DC, 1884)

Goodwin, John, *The Pilgrim Republic* (Boston, 1888)

Gookin, Daniel, *An Historical Account of the Indians* (Whitefish, MA, 2003)

Grigson, Jane, *Jane Grigson's Fish Book* (London, 1993)

Haro, A. T. et al., 'Simulated Effects of Hydroelectric Project Regulation on Mortality of American Eels', *American Fisheries Society Symposium* (2003), pp. 357–65

Helfman, Gene S., 'Spinning for their Supper', *Natural History* (May 1995), pp. 26–9

Jacobs, Francine, *The Freshwater Eel* (New York, 1973)

Jacoby, Leopold, *The Eel Question* (Washington, DC, 1882)

Jesse, Edward, *Gleanings in Natural History* (London, 1834)

Jones, Evan, *American Food: The Gastronomic Story* (Woodstock, NY, 1990)

Josselyn, John, *Two Voyages To New England* (Cambridge, 1833)

Katoh, Masaya and Masahiro Kobayashi, 'Aquaculture and Genetic Structure in the Japanese Eel, Anguilla Japonica', *US.-Japan Cooperative Program in Natural Resources Technical Report No. 30* (2000), p. 87

Knights, B., 'A Review of the Possible Impacts of Long-Term Oceanic and Climate Changes and Fishing Mortality on Recruitment of Anguillid Eels of the Northern Hemisphere', *Science of the Total Environment* (2003), pp. 237–44

Lamothe, Peter et al., 'Homing and Movement of Yellow-Phase American Eels in Freshwater Ponds', *Environmental Biology of Fishes*, LVIII (2000), pp. 393–9

Mayhew, Henry, *London Labour and the London Poor*, vol. I (London, 1861)

McKenzie, Clyde Jr, *The Fisheries of Raritan Bay* (New Brunswick, NJ, 1992)

Moriarty, Christopher, *Eels: A Natural and Unnatural History* (New York, 1978)

Ohta, Hiromi, 'Artificial Fertilization Using Testicular Spermatozoa in the Japanese Eel Anguilla Japonica', *Fisheries Science*, LXIII/3 (1997), pp. 393–6

Oppianus, *Halieuticks of the Nature of Fishes* trans. John Jones, Book I (Oxford, 1722)

Ottolenghi, Francesca et al., *Capture-Based Aquaculture* (Rome, 2004)

Parker, S. J., 'Homing Ability and Home Range of Yellow-Phase American Eels in a Tidally Dominated Estuary', *Journal of Marine Biological Association UK* (1995), pp. 127–40

Pennisi, Elizabeth, 'Much Ado about Eels', *BioScience* (1989), p. 596

Radcliffe, William, *Fishing from the Earliest Times* (Chicago, IL, 1974)

Randolph, Mary, *The Virginia Housewife* (Washington, DC, 1824)

Root, Waverly, *Food* (New York, 1980)

Sagard-Theodat, Gabriel, *The Long Journey to the Country of the Hurons*

(Toronto, 1939)

Schmidt, Johannes, *The Breeding Places of the Eel* (Washington, DC, 1924)

Schmit, Julie et al., 'Chinese Fish Crisis Shows Seafood Safety Challenges', *USA Today* (Money) (28 June 2007)

Schweid, Richard, *Consider the Eel* (Cambridge, MA, 2004)

Smith, Jim, *Pie 'n' Mash: A Guide To London's Traditional Eating Houses* (London, 1995)

Speck, Frank, *Penobscot Man* (Philadelphia, 1940)

Sullivan, M. C. et al., '*Anguilla Rostrata* Glass Eel Ingress into Two US East Coast Estuaries: Patterns, Processes and Implications for Adult Eel Abundance', *Journal of Fish Biology* (2006), pp. 1081–101.

Swift, Graham, *Waterland* (New York, 1983)

Tanaka, H. et al., 'The First Production of Glass Eel in Captivity: Fish Reproductive Physiology Facilitates Great Progress in Aquaculture', *Fish Physiology and Biochemistry*, XXVIII/1–4 (2003), pp. 493–7

Tesch, Friedrich-Wilhelm, *The Eel* (London, 1977)

—— 'The Sargasso Sea Expedition, 1979', *Helgoländer Meeresuntersuchungen*, XXXV (1982), pp. 263–77

Walton, Izaak and Charles Cotton, *The Compleat Angler* (London, 1960)

Wood, William, *New England's Prospect* (Amherst, MA, 1993)

Wynken de Worde, *Book of Saint Albans* (1496), trans. William Van Wyck (New York, 1933)

Associations and Websites

ATLANTIC STATES MARINE FISHERIES COMMISSION
www.asmfc.org/americanEel.htm

'FISH INEQUITIES'
www.glooskapandthefrog.org/Eel.htm

GULF OF MAINE COUNCIL ON THE MARINE ENVIRONMENT
www.gulfofmaine.org/council/publication/American_eel_high-res.pdf

INTERNATIONAL COUNCIL FOR THE EXPLORATION OF THE SEA
www.ices.dk/marineworld/eel.asp

NATIONAL ANGUILLA CLUB
www.nationalanguillaclub.co.uk

UK GLASS EELS
www.glasseel.com

US FISH & WILDLIFE SERVICE
www.fws.gov/northeast/ameel/

Acknowledgements

Heartfelt thanks to my *sorella anguilla*, Victòria Rabal i Merola, for her encouragement of, and help with, this book. And to all those around the world who are doing their best to ensure the survival of freshwater eels. Books are collaborative efforts and my gratitude goes out to all the people and libraries that have provided me with information about eels over the years. While many sources helped bring this book into being, any errors therein are wholly my responsibility.

Photo Acknowledgements

The author and publishers wish to express their thanks to the below sources of illustrative material and/or permission to reproduce it. (Some sources uncredited in the captions for reasons of brevity are also given below.)

Photo Achilles2k/BigStockPhoto: p. 110; photos akg-images: pp. 79, 82; photos akg-images/Erich Lessing: pp. 71, 156; photos author: pp. 20, 26, 90, 91, 129, 143, 144, 150, 157; Bodleian Library, University of Oxford (MS Douce 360, f. 33r): p. 154 (foot); photo Arne Bramsen/BigStock-Photo: p. 72; from A. E. Brehm, *Brehms Tierleben. . .* vol. II (Leipzig, 1915): p. 56; British Library, London: pp. 23, 140; photo A. Bruni/Alinari/Rex Features: p. 61; from David Cairncross, *The Origin of the Silver Eel, with Remarks on Bait and Fly Fishing* (London, 1892): p. 46; from Folco Cecchini, *Sorella Anguilla* (Nuova Alfa editoriale, Bologna, 1990): pp. 57, 58, 59, 86; photos courtesy of the Comacchio Tourist Board: pp. 87, 89; from Alexandre Dumas' *Grand Dictionaire de Cuisine* (Paris, 1873): pp. 73, 94; Collection of the Fenimore Art Museum, Cooperstown, New York (gift of Stephen C. Clark; photo courtesy New York State Historical Association): p. 155; photo © Thomas Flügge/2009 iStock International Inc.: p. 12; Gavà Museum, Catalonia, Spain: p. 117; photo Ronald Hudson/BigStockPhoto: p. 37; from J. J. Kaup, *Catalogue of Apodal Fish in the Collection of the British Museum* (London, 1856): p. 28; Koninklijke Bibliotheek, The Hague: p. 80; from the Larousse Gastronomique (Paris, 1938): p. 112; photo © Jay Lazarin/2009 iStock International Inc.: p. 115; photo Library of Congress, Washington, DC:

p. 104; photo © Maher/2009 iStock International Inc.: p. 16; photos Victòria Rabal i Merola: pp. 99, 136, 158; Musée des Beaux-Arts, Carpentras: p. 82; Musée des Beaux-Arts de la Ville de Paris, Petit Palais (photo © Petit Palais/Roger-Viollet/Rex Features): p. 95; Musée Carnavalet, Paris (photo © Musée Carnavalet/ Roger-Viollet/Rex Features): p. 92; National Gallery, London: p. 84; photo Rex Features: p. 64; photos © Roger-Viollet/Rex Features: pp. 125, 127; photo Mark Salt, courtesy National Anguilla Club http://www.nationalanguillaclub. co.uk/: p. 111; from J. Schmidt, 'The Breeding Places of the Eel', *Annual Report of the Smithsonian Institution* (1924): pp. 31, 38, 39, 132, 133; from Gotthilf Heinrich von Schubert, *Naturgeschichte* (Munich, 1890): p. 8; photo Sinopix Photo Agency Ltd/Rex Features: p. 11; photo Sipa Press/ Rex Features: p. 64; photo © Sotheby's/akg-images: p. 85; photo © Len Tillim/2009 iStock International Inc.: p. 36; photo Jonna Tomkiewicz, DTU Aqua, Technical University of Denmark, Charlottenlund: p. 18; photo L. Torstensson/IBL/Rex Features: p. 147; photo Undy/ BigStockPhoto: p. 126; photo © Frank van Haalen/2009 iStock International Inc.: p. 122 (top); photo © Duncan Walker/2009 iStock International Inc.: p. 118; photo Warburg Institute, London: p. 154 (top); photo © webstuff/2009 iStock International Inc.: p. 6; Werner Forman Archive: p. 60; from Francis Willughby, *De Historia Piscium. . .* (Oxford, 1686): p. 40; from J. G. Wood, *The Illustrated Natural History* (London, 1863): pp. 41, 48, 49, 52; photo Kenny Yeoh/BigStockPhoto: p. 138; photos © Zoological Society of London: pp. 28, 40, 48, 49, 52.

Index